Politics and Affect in Black Women's Fiction

Philosophy of Race

Series Editor: George Yancy, Emory University

Editorial Board: Sybol Anderson, Barbara Applebaum, Alison Bailey, Chike Jeffers, Janine Jones, David Kim, Emily S. Lee, Zeus Leonardo, Falguni A. Sheth, Grant Silva

The Philosophy of Race book series publishes interdisciplinary projects that center upon the concept of race, a concept that continues to have very profound contemporary implications. Philosophers and other scholars, more generally, are strongly encouraged to submit book projects that seriously address race and the process of racialization as a deeply embodied, existential, political, social, and historical phenomenon. The series is open to examine monographs, edited collections, and revised dissertations that critically engage the concept of race from multiple perspectives: sociopolitical, feminist, existential, phenomenological, theological, and historical.

Titles in the Series

White Self-Criticality beyond Anti-racism, edited by George Yancy
The Post-Racial Limtis of Memorialization: Toward a Political Sense of Mourning, edited by Tina Fernandes Botts
The Habits of Racism: A Phenomenology of Racism and Racialized Embodiment, by Helen Ngo
Politics and Affect in Black Women's Fiction, by Kathy Glass

Politics and Affect in Black Women's Fiction

Kathy Glass

LEXINGTON BOOKS
Lanham • Boulder • New York • London

Published by Lexington Books
An imprint of The Rowman & Littlefield Publishing Group, Inc.
4501 Forbes Boulevard, Suite 200, Lanham, Maryland 20706
www.rowman.com

Unit A, Whitacre Mews, 26-34 Stannary Street, London SE11 4AB

Copyright © 2018 by Lexington Books

Excerpts from *From Caucasia With Love* © Senna, Danzy, September 19, 2013 and Bloomsbury Publishing Plc.

Portions of chapter 3 are reprinted with permission from Glass, Kathy, "Nella Larsen's Spiritual Strivings," *A Companion to the Harlem Renaissance*, John Wiley & Sons Ltd.

Excerpt(s) from CAUCASIA: A NOVEL by Danzy Senna, copyright © 1998 by Danzy Senna. Used by permission of Riverhead, an imprint of Penguin Publishing Group, a division of Penguin Random House LLC. All rights reserved.

All rights reserved. No part of this book may be reproduced in any form or by any electronic or mechanical means, including information storage and retrieval systems, without written permission from the publisher, except by a reviewer who may quote passages in a review.

British Library Cataloguing in Publication Information Available

Library of Congress Cataloging-in-Publication Data Available

ISBN 978-1-4985-3839-8 (cloth : alk. paper)
ISBN 978-1-4985-3840-4 (electronic)

∞™ The paper used in this publication meets the minimum requirements of American National Standard for Information Sciences Permanence of Paper for Printed Library Materials, ANSI/NISO Z39.48-1992.

Printed in the United States of America

Contents

Acknowledgments ix
Introduction 1

1 Love-Driven Politics in Frances Harper's "The Two Offers" 11
2 "Do Unto Others": De-Racializing the Golden Rule in Julia Collins's *The Curse of Caste; or The Slave Bride* 33
3 Nella Larsen's Spiritual Strivings 61
4 On Blackness and Longing in Danzy Senna's *Caucasia* 81

Conclusion 105
Bibliography 111
Index 119
About the Author 125

Acknowledgments

I am very grateful to Jana Hodges-Kluck for supporting this project. Professor George Yancy, a superb scholar, teacher, and mentor, also deserves heartfelt thanks for his encouragement and longtime support of my work. In addition, I am grateful for the anonymous external reviewer's thoughtful reading and insightful response to my book.

Next, I want to extend warm thanks to Daniel P. Watkins, who read various versions of this text, for his invaluable feedback and insight. I am also grateful for Duquesne University colleagues for support and assistance, including Dean James Swindal, Greg Barnhisel, Daniel Burston, Timothy Vincent, and graduate student Alexandra Reznik. Thanks, also, to Joycelyn Moody, Linda Kinnahan, and Emad Mirmotahari, who read and responded to a portion of this book in its embryonic stage. I would also like to thank George Lipsitz and David Kim, who organized the "Love-Driven Politics" symposium in the "City of Brotherly Love," for fueling my imagination and expanding my thinking on love's political possibilities.

Also, heartfelt thanks to my husband, Brent, for his constant encouragement and inspiration, and deep thanks to my parents, who first kindled my love of reading and encouraged my writing. Warm thanks to my sister, Beverly, for her enduring love and encouragement; additionally, I am grateful for Eva Roberts (across the miles) and Joseph Kennedy III, whose unflagging support has blessed me beyond measure.

In addition, I thank Wiley-Blackwell for permission to use copyrighted material. Chapter 3 is a modified version of "Nella Larsen's Spiritual Strivings" published in the Wiley-Blackwell *Companion to the Harlem Renaissance,* edited by Cherene Sherrard-Johnson. Copyright 2015, John Wiley & Sons, Ltd. All rights reserved. No part of this publication may be reproduced, stored in a retrieval system, or transmitted, in any form or by any means, electronic, mechanical, photocopying, recording or otherwise, except as permitted by the UK Copyright, Designs and Patents Act 1988, without the prior permission of the publisher.

Introduction

In an interview with *The New Yorker*, Toni Morrison says that "[b]eing a black woman writer is not a shallow place but a rich place to write from." Significantly, she adds, "[i]t doesn't limit my imagination; it expands it."[1] Exploring literary possibilities, this book reads black women's texts as richly creative documents saturated with sociopolitical value. I am specifically interested in the ways that African American women fiction writers from the nineteenth century to the present have mined the politics of affect and emotion to document love, shame, and suffering in environments shaped by race. Examining existential blackness and affective responses to social injustice in literature also allows me to consider how black women writers deploy emotional states to move readers to progressive political action. These concerns are important because affect creates powerful contexts for individual and collective acts of sociopolitical resistance.

Love and social change are not new topics in African American Studies. Towering activist-writers Dr. Martin Luther King, Jr. and James Baldwin, and prolific scholars Frances Smith Foster,[2] Melba Joyce Boyd,[3] Joycelyn K. Moody,[4] DoVeanna Fulton,[5] bell hooks,[6] and Tess Chakkalakal[7] all generate keen insights into the sociopolitical dynamics of love in black communities; my project is indebted to and engages this rich tradition of African American activism and scholarship. *Politics and Affect in Black Women's Fiction* also builds upon African American women writers' broader philosophical and political commitments to sociopolitical concerns. In the nineteenth century, for example, activists like Maria W. Stewart, Anna Julia Cooper, and Frances Harper,[8] denied inclusion in the raced and gendered category of citizen, contested narrow constructions of citizenship and the racial state in which it was grounded. Throughout the twentieth century, black women continued to problematize their marginalized political position, critiquing classism, racism, sexism, and homophobia.[9] The struggle continues, as black women in the twenty-first century engage philosophical questions about what it means to be black and female in a nation where they are "treated as virtually invisible"[10] in corporate America, and garner less attention than men in the Black Lives Matter movement.[11] While my literary study examines the particularities of love and blackness, it will also take up broader questions of race, sexuality, gender, citizenship, and visibility, as they intersect with black women's literary texts.

Focusing specifically on black women's philosophy of love in this study, I use affect and reader-response theory, alternatively and jointly, to explore the ways Frances Harper's "The Two Offers" (1859), Julia Collins's *The Curse of Caste* (1865), Nella Larsen's *Quicksand* (1928), and Danzy Senna's *Caucasia* (1998) evoke a distinct love-based, antiracist, antisexist politics of compassion. Not only do these works theorize a philosophy of love but they also resist structures of domination that reflect what bell hooks terms a "white-supremacist capitalist patriarchy."[12] The following chapters will examine how these four African American women writers represent black suffering and invite reader empathy and self-examination in relation to the pain documented. I will also show how black women writers valorize compassion and social action as responses to pain. Arguably, these African American writers emphasize black humanity, promote political responses to black suffering, and encourage reader resistance to sociopolitical oppression. I will use both reader-response and affect theory to investigate historical responses to black texts and gauge potential responses to black bodies in literary works. Displaying an antiracist ethos, these stories ask readers to "tarry"[13] in affective states that could move them to progressive social action.

METHODOLOGY

Eve Kosofsky Sedgwick's groundbreaking *Touching Feeling* offers a comprehensive look at the emergence and development of affect studies,[14] while Anne Cvetkovich's seminal *An Archive of Feelings* highlights affect, queer trauma, and lesbian identity.[15] Both are foundational studies in affect theory yet neither gives sustained attention to race. Lauren Berlant's *The Female Complaint: The Unfinished Business of Sentimentality in American Culture* does the critical work of "[t]racking mass-mediated norms of belonging in the affective register and conventions of engendering emotional solidarities" which "helps us to understand the reproduction of normative life amid serious doubts about the probability that anyone, except the lucky, will be able to forge durable relations of reciprocity among intimates or strangers."[16] Berlant's compelling study attends to race, class, and gender as it focuses on a range of "early twentieth-century fictions and their filmic adaptations, whose main gaze is at the United States, at white women, at liberal hetero-femininity, fantasy, and love."[17] Given my focus on black women's cultural production, I want to extend the theoretical interest of Sedgwick, Cvetkovich, and Berlant by placing it alongside Rebecca Wanzo's *The Suffering Will Not Be Televised*,[18] which explores how race privilege historically renders white female bodies as eligible for public sympathy in the media, while putting under erasure similarly situated black female bodies. Wanzo's impressive study examines the effectivity of black women's sentimental storytelling practices, and their ability to exert "affective agency" in both literary texts and in the mass media.[19] Unlike Wanzo's book, my study focuses exclusively on black women's literature and draws insights from Sara Ahmed's *The Cultural Politics of Emotion*, which examines, in part, "the emotionality of texts in terms of the way in which texts name or perform different emotions."[20] Further, I am interested in how the written word produces meaning and promotes action through philosophical narratives and rhetorical strategies. While literature provides the object of inquiry, questions of literariness are situated among the historical and social contexts in which literature is embedded.

Some proponents of affect theory argue its value lies partly in its ability to overcome philosophical dualisms detrimental to nuanced studies of literature and lived experience. As Cvetkovich explains, "the affective turn takes up debates about the construction of binary oppositions between reason and emotion and the reversal of hierarchies that subordinate emotion to reason as part of a mind/body split often associated with the seventeenth-century philosopher René Descartes."[21] Aligned with these goals, Sedgwick positions her key study on affect as "a project to explore promising tools and techniques for nondualistic thought and pedagogy."[22] Relatedly, Jane Thrailkill writes that "[n]ew work in a variety of fields, including . . . affect theory . . . provides a set of tools for recovering the ways that literary realists, along with their contemporaries in philosophy and the emergent sciences of the body, actively challenged a number of conceptual divisions that had been central to the Western philosophical tradition."[23] As dualisms separating the mind/body and realism/sentimentalism serve to "structure and to limit our critical conversations about literary realism and, more broadly, the ends of literary studies,"[24] I join Thrailkill and others who have a sustained and varied history of challenging binaristic thinking.[25]

Black women writers and critics have an identifiable tradition of disturbing disempowering dualisms (mind/body, reason/emotion, black/white) and engaging black lived experience. Maria W. Stewart, Anna Julia Cooper, Pauline Hopkins, Barbara Christian, Audre Lorde, bell hooks, and Toni Morrison among others reflect a tradition of creativity and intellectualism serving to overturn binary categories that would elide, suppress, and deny black complexity. Attending to "critical chronologies" in "Invoking Affect," Clare Hemmings stresses that we must identify the "vast range of epistemological work that attends to emotional investments, political connectivity and the possibility of change," as this critical labor prepared the way for the widely celebrated "turn to affect."[26] Hemmings proceeds to identify as a prime example feminist standpoint, and its "key proponents [who] range across Marxist, feminism, critical race theory, sexual difference theory, as well as poststructuralism."[27] The writers appearing in the following pages similarly engage the "relationship between the ontological, epistemological and transformative" and as such, this project will take a holistic approach to black literature examining affect and social action, paying close attention to the impact of emotional life on the mind, body, and social world.[28]

While affect theory frames my study, I consciously privilege literature over theory, using the latter to illuminate key themes in the former. I engage affect theory in *Politics and Affect* not to obscure the important subject of love in black women's literature but rather to use a framework that addresses "intensities of feeling, emotional attachments and gut reactions."[29] Moreover, affect theory offers useful frameworks to consider how, as Ahmed puts it, "what we do is shaped by the contact we have with others."[30] As a relational model for understanding human experience, affect studies foreground questions deeply embedded in interpersonal relations, emotional states, and racially charged environments. Interested in the possibilities of human agency, I read fictive subjects as "embodied subjects" bearing the capacity to resist and even "exceed social subjection."[31] Examining affect and emotion, I further draw on reader-response theory to explore how writers in my study position readers to encounter and be transformed by the powerful embodied states inscribed in their texts.

Theorist Wolfgang Iser writes, "[i]n the act of reading, having to think something that we have not yet experienced does not mean only being in a position to conceive or even understand it; it also means that such acts of conception are possible and successful to the degree that they lead to something being formulated in us."[32] The texts in my study present readers with opportunities to comprehend and identify with representations of black life, but they go further, endeavoring to "stimulate attitudes" in diverse reading audiences capable of enacting social change.[33] Representations of dehumanized slaves; depictions of racist encounters; and portrayals of racist affect in these narratives serve to educate readers, but as the following chapters show, these textual moments can also affect readers and present alternative frameworks for engaging difference.

A highly contested term, affect resists closure and carries multiple meanings in critical scholarship. I will not attempt here a comprehensive review of affect studies and its cross-disciplinary trajectories but will establish a working definition of affect and identify areas of the field most useful to my project. In *The Transmission of Affect,* Teresa Brennan argues that affect is the "physiological shift accompanying a judgment."[34] She goes on to suggest "the things that one feels are affects. The things that one feels with are feelings."[35] Similarly exploring the link between affects and related phenomena, Hemmings distinguishes between emotions and affect, as the latter "broadly refers to states of being, rather than to their manifestation or interpretation as emotions."[36] Brian Massumi and Lawrence Goldberg further assert that "emotion requires a subject while affect does not" and "that the former designates feeling given 'function and meaning' while the latter remains 'unformed and unstructured.'"[37]

Reflecting on such distinctions in *Ugly Feelings,* Sianne Ngai writes that she "will not be theoretically leaning on [the distinction between affect and emotion] to the extent that others have—as may be apparent from the way in which [she] use[s] the two terms more or less interchangeably."[38] Ngai does not insist on these distinctions, in part, since

> [a]t the end of the day, the difference between emotion and affect is still intended to solve the same basic and fundamentally descriptive problem it was coined in psychoanalytic practice to solve: that of distinguishing first-person from third-person feeling, and, by extension, feeling that is contained by an identity from feeling that is not.[39]

Ngai articulates a persuasive case for using "affect" and "emotion" interchangeably, as does Cvetkovich, who avers that affect "names a conceptual problem as much as a tangible thing. As such, it is best understood as an umbrella term that includes related, and more familiar, words such as 'feeling' and 'emotion,' as well as efforts to make distinctions among them."[40] Following Ngai and Cvetkovich, I use both affect and emotion to name and examine the constellation of feelings, affects, and emotions made manifest in black women's literature, often overlapping, intersecting, and resisting theoretical frameworks.

This book engages a specific thread of affect studies amplified by Sedgwick and Adam Frank, who published in 1995 a volume of writings by American psychologist Silvan Tomkins (1911–1991).[41] In particular, Sedgwick and Frank note how Tomkins's work on affect enables a shift away from "the Freudian emphasis on oedipality and repression" and they further claim that his "resistance to heterosexist teleologies is founded in the most basic terms of his understanding of affect."[42] More recently, Melissa Gregg and Gregory J. Seigworth have named 1995 as the "watershed moment" for affect studies as in that year, "two essays— one by Eve Sedgwick and Adam Frank ("Shame in the Cybernetic Fold" [a version of which also appears in the 1995 published volume] and one by Brian Massumi ("The Autonomy of Affect") were published."[43] Gregg and Seigworth associate these affect theorists with "the two dominant vectors of affect study in the humanities: Silvan Tomkins's psychobiology of differential affects . . . and Gilles Deleuze's Spinozist ethology of bodily capacities."[44] While Tomkins is known for differentiating between affects and drives, as well as for breaking down affects into specific components, Deleuze "understands affect as describing the passage from one state to another, as an *intensity* characterized by an increase or decrease in power."[45] For the purposes of this project, Tomkins's framework proves more useful as it elaborates a distinct set of affects and connects them to outward behavior.

Specifically, Tomkins (1911–1991) writes that basic affects include interest-excitement, enjoyment-joy, surprise-startle, distress-anguish, fear-terror, shame-humiliation, contempt-disgust, and anger-rage.[46] For Tomkins, affect is a "motivational system in human beings" that connects states of being with behavior.[47] According to psychiatrist Paul C. Holinger, "affects combine with each other and with any form of experience to become our *complex emotional life*."[48] *Politics and Affect* draws on Tomkins's basic affect model to isolate specific physiological responses to stimuli and examine the "complex emotional life" detailed in black women's fiction. In particular, this study pinpoints how love, distress, shame, fear, and terror intertwine with sociopolitical life in black women's fiction, and further examines how affect both creates and undermines empowering communal bonds that enable resistance to oppression.

Politics and Affect offers original readings of classic and contemporary black texts that raise sociopolitical concerns central to my study. Namely, I am interested in the pain that racism spawns and love-based, antiracist strategies of resistance. Ample criticism exists on Harper's "The Two Offers," for example, but my study highlights the antiracist politics of love compelling the heroine's sociopolitical activism in the narrative. Also critical to my study, Collins's *The Curse of Caste* represents black suffering and critiques white supremacy. Much of the scholarship on this serialized novel explores black periodical culture, biraciality, memory, and sentimental storytelling practices. I, too, engage these key issues, but my book gives sustained attention to the radical love positioned as political and antiracist in the novel. *Quicksand* and *Caucasia* enrich my project further, poignantly representing black pain and documenting the impact of racist affect on the black body. Each text in my study emphasizes black humanity and encourages reader identification with the black body. While a range of affects run through all four literary works, love connects and informs each text. Love, in my study, builds on bell hooks's observation that "to truly love we must learn to mix various ingredients—care, affection, recognition, respect, commitment, and trust, as well as honest and open communication."[49] Highlighting practices of loving the self and others in black women's fiction, this book necessarily attends to the vulnerability and rejection one risks in intimate encounters.

THE CHAPTERS

While Collins's and Harper's antebellum texts explore love in the context of slavery, Larsen's and Senna's novels examine love's power in an ostensibly "free" period marred by racial violence and pervasive inequality. Larsen's *Quicksand*, for example, documents the realities of lynching and Jim Crow, while Senna's *Caucasia* details the cultural and structural racism plaguing post-Civil Rights America. Despite political victories that promised African Americans formal equality before the law, questions of love (individual and social) remain fraught with racial injustice and threats of violence in these writings. Examined together, each work becomes an important case study on love's risks and restorative power in black women's literature, offering rich insight into black culture inscribed in literary texts.

The first chapter focuses on Frances Harper's "The Two Offers," a sentimental short story that rewrites and radicalizes the nineteenth-century discourse of true womanhood. As black feminist scholarship shows,[50] Harper's story complicates conventional sentimental narratives by challenging narrow gender roles relegating women to the domestic sphere, asserting the dignity of the fugitive slave, and promoting the value of antislavery activism. I call attention, however, to what I term an antiracist politics of love undergirding Harper's story, and suggest "The Two Offers" delineates a love-based philosophy born of suffering that connects its protagonist Janette to community activism, thereby enjoining its readers to engage in similar forms of sociopolitical action. Dwelling with the affect of distress and positing the value of sentiment, this chapter highlights the politics of affect and subversive acts of love.

The following chapter contemplates love alongside affective distress and rage in a second sentimental text—Julia Collins's *The Curse of Caste*. I argue that Collins's novel challenges racist ideology by rendering visible the tragic consequences (psychic and material) of white supremacist values infesting the nation. In particular, I investigate the death and trauma resulting from white violence enacted against enslaved women. Ultimately, I assert that Collins's sentimental aesthetic endorses alternative epistemologies and advocates the radicalization of love in the form of "the Golden Rule."[51] In its exploration of racial injustice and healing, *The Curse* suggests the difficulty of racial reconciliation pending a conscious national divestment from whiteness—as a dominant structure of social and political authority—and a wholesale reconsideration of "race" in the U.S. imaginary.

Chapter 3 notes love's elusiveness in Nella Larsen's modern novels *Quicksand* and *Passing*. Burdened by a bevy of forces in the modern world, Helga Crane, the mixed-raced and middle-class protagonist in *Quicksand,* feels alienated from both herself and the black community. Her embodied states of despair, lack, and longing drive her from the southern to the northern U.S., to Scandinavia, and back to the American South, in search of fulfillment. As her locale shifts, Helga navigates affective shame (given her sexual longings as a woman) and disgust (arising from internalized racism). Arguably, these burdensome states shape her lived experience and alter her destiny. Chapter 3 argues that Helga's search for fulfillment is also a search for compassion. Additionally, I propose that in *Passing,* Larsen further explores questions of black female agency and spirituality in the early twentieth century. Like Helga, protagonist Irene Redfield lives a spiritually barren life in middle-class surroundings. Desperately insecure, Irene longs for stability and turns to religion to assuage her fears. Examining both Helga's and Irene's superficial forays into religiosity, I suggest that Larsen critiques their uncritical engagement with spirituality, and emphasizes their lack of agency as black women in the U.S. Using Brennan's reading of contagious affect,[52] this chapter also explores how "racist affect" is transferred between bodies, and how affect engenders social acts in both narratives. Analyzing affective shame, despair, excitement, and rage, I hope to shed further light on Helga's and Irene's race- and gender-inflected plight in the modern world.

Chapter 4 highlights a mixed-raced young woman navigating the late twentieth-century racial terrain in the U.S. Like Helga Crane in *Quicksand*, the protagonist Birdie Lee in Danzy Senna's *Caucasia* is a biracial woman who self-identifies as black. A culturally African American girl in a phenotypically white body, Birdie attends a predominantly black school as a child, and a virtually all-white school as a teen. Throughout her early years, she alternatively longs for blackness, invisibility, visibility, and love. I examine Birdie's longings and argue for love's centrality in the novel. At the same time, I explore affective distress and shame in racialized space, and the emotional impact of antiblack discourse on Birdie's white's body. Further, I suggest that *Caucasia* delineates the narrator's evolving and increasingly politicized voice, which critiques the reproduction of whiteness and its psychic consequences across racial lines.

My concluding section examines the affective and philosophical threads connecting each chapter, and the evolution of radical love across the writings of Harper, Collins, Larsen, and Senna. In bringing together these black women's texts, I do not mean to minimize their formal, thematic, and historical differences. Rather, in bringing them together, I illuminate a diverse set of texts that challenge racism and variously testify to love's social and political value. More specifically, each work highlights the damage (psychic and/or somatic) that racism wreaks, and contributes to a broader politics emphasizing the need for compassion in personal and political contexts. While the literary works discussed in this book cannot stand in for the entirety of African American letters, read in tandem they comprise key philosophical reflections on love's sociopolitical power, an understudied yet urgent topic requiring sustained attention in the African American literary tradition.

NOTES

1. Hilton Als, "Ghosts in the House: How Toni Morrison Fostered a Generation of Black Writers," *New Yorker*, October 27, 2003, accessed May 5, 2017. http://www.newyorker.com/magazine/2003/10/27/ghosts-in-the-house.

2. See Frances Smith Foster, *Love and Marriage in Early African America* (Lebanon: Northeastern UP, 2008).

3. Melba Joyce Boyd, *Discarded Legacy: Politics and Poetics in the Life of Frances E.W. Harper, 1825–1911* (Detroit: Wayne State, 1994).

4. Joycelyn K. Moody, "Ripping Away the Veil of Slavery: Literacy, Communal Love, and Self Esteem in Three Slave Women's Narratives," *Black American Literature Forum* 24(4), 1990, 633–48.

5. DoVeanna S. Fulton, *Speaking Power: Black Feminist Orality in Women's Narratives of Slavery* (Albany: State University of New York Press, 2006).

6. bell hooks, *Salvation: Black People and Love* (New York: Perennial, 2001).

7. Tess Chakkalakal, *Novel Bondage: Slavery, Marriage, and Freedom in Nineteenth-Century America* (Urbana: University of Illinois Press, 2011).

8. See Beverly Guy-Sheftall, ed., *Words of Fire: An Anthology of African-American Feminist Thought* (New York: New York Press, 1995), esp. 25–33; 39–42, 43–49.

9. See, for example, Demita Frazier, Barbara Smith, and Beverly Smith, "The Combahee River Collective" in *Words of Fire*, 231–40.

10. Valerie Purdie-Vaughns. Commentary. "Why So Few Black Women Are Senior Managers in 2015." Fortune.com. Time Inc. Network, April 2015. Web. 17 June 2015.

11. See "#Say Her Name Report." African American Policy Forum, Web. 17 June 2015.

12. hooks, *Salvation*, 143.

13. See George Yancy, *Look, A White!: Philosophical Essays on Whiteness* (Philadelphia: Temple University Press, 2012), 140.

14. Eve K. Sedgwick, *Touching Feeling: Affect, Pedagogy, Performativity* (Durham: Duke University Press, 2003).

15. Ann Cvetkovich, *An Archive of Feelings: Trauma, Sexuality, and Lesbian Public Cultures* (Durham: Duke University Press, 2003).

16. Lauren Berlant, *The Female Complaint: The Unfinished Business of Sentimentality in American Culture* (Durham: Duke University Press, 2008), 22.

17. Berlant, *The Female Complaint*, 23.

18. Rebecca Wanzo, *The Suffering Will Not Be Televised: African American Women and Sentimental Political Storytelling* (New York: SUNY, 2009).

19. Wanzo, *The Suffering*, 3.

20. Sara Ahmed, *The Cultural Politics of Emotion* (New York: Routledge, 2004), 13.

21. See Cvetkovich, "Affect" in *Keywords for American Cultural Studies*, ed. Bruce Burgett et al. Second Edition (New York: New York University Press, 2007), 13.

22. Sedgwick, "Introduction," *Touching Feeling*, 1.

23. See Jane Thrailkill, *Affecting Fictions: Mind, Body, and Emotion in American Literary Realism* (Cambridge: Harvard University Press, 2007), 10.

24. Thrailkill, *Affecting Fictions*, 10.

25. See, for example, Angela Y. Davis, *The Meaning of Freedom* (San Francisco: City Lights, 2012); George Yancy, *Black Bodies, White Gazes: The Continuing Significance of Race* (Lanham: Rowman and Littlefield, 2008); and Cornel West, *The Cornel West Reader* (New York: Basic Civitas, 1999).

26. See Clare Hemmings, "Invoking Affect: Cultural Theory and the Ontological Turn," *Cultural Studies* 19(5), 2005, 557.

27. Hemmings, "Invoking Affect," 557–58.

28. Hemmings, "Invoking Affect," 557.

29. See Marianne Liljestrom and Susanna Paasonen, introduction, "Feeling Differences—Affect and Feminist Reading" in *Working with Affect in Feminist Readings* (New York: Routledge), 1.

30. Ahmed, *The Cultural Politics of Emotion*, 4.

31. Hemmings, "Invoking Affect," 549.

32. Wolfgang Iser, "The Reading Process: A Phenomenological Approach" in *Reader-Response Criticism: From Formalism to Post-Structuralism*, ed. Jane P. Tompkins (Baltimore: The Johns Hopkins University Press, 1980), 67.

33. Iser, *The Reading Process*, 65
34. Teresa Brennan, *The Transmission of Affect* (Ithaca: Cornell, 2004), 5.
35. Brennan, *The Transmission of Affect*, 23.
36. Hemmings, "Invoking Affect," 551.
37. Qtd. in Sianne Ngai, *Ugly Feelings* (Cambridge: Harvard University Press, 2005), 25.
38. Ngai, *Ugly Feelings*, 27.
39. Ngai, *Ugly Feelings*, 27.
40. See Cvetkovich, "Affect," 13.
41. See *Shame and Its Sisters: A Silvan Tomkins Reader*, ed. Eve Sedgwick et al. (Durham: Duke University Press, 1995).
42. Sedgwick and Frank, eds., *Shame and Its Sisters*, 6, 7.
43. Melissa Gregg and Gregory J. Seigworth, "An Inventory of Shimmers" in *The Affect Theory Reader* (Durham, Duke University Press, 2010), 5.
44. Gregg and Seigworth, "An Inventory of Shimmers," 5.
45. Hemmings, "Invoking Affect," 552 (original emphasis).
46. Sedgwick and Frank, eds.,"What Are Affects?" in *Shame and Its Sisters: A Silvan Tomkins Reader*, 74.
47. See Sedgwick and Frank, eds., *Shame and Its Sisters*, 34.
48. Paul C. Holinger, "Silvan S. Tomkins, 1911–1991." *Dr. Paul C. Holinger's Place for Parents and Children*. n.d. Web. 7 July 2014. Emphasis mine.
49. bell hooks, *All About Love* (New York: Perennial, 2000), 5.
50. See, for example, Carla Peterson, *Doers of the Word* (New York: Oxford University Press, 1995); and Ann duCille, *The Coupling Convention* (New York: Oxford University Press, 1993).
51. See Julia Collins, *The Curse of Caste* (New York: Oxford UP, 2006), 132.
52. See Brennan, *The Transmission of Affect*.

ONE
Love-Driven Politics in Frances Harper's "The Two Offers"

In "Our Greatest Want" (1859), Frances Ellen Watkins Harper (1825–1911) identifies the black community's most urgent needs: "If I understand our greatest wants aright they strike deeper than any want that gold or knowledge can supply. We want more soul, a higher cultivation of all our spiritual faculties. We need more unselfishness, earnestness and integrity."[1] Embracing spiritual values, Harper invites her African American readers of the *Anglo African Magazine* to cultivate, tend, and share their inner resources. In the concluding line she proclaims, "[t]he important lesson we should learn and be able to teach, is how to make every gift, whether gold or talent, fortune or genius, subserve the cause of crushed humanity."[2] Widening her message to rally every possible resource for the oppressed, Harper pens a passionate call for soulful, other-directed men and women willing to circulate spiritual and material offerings to benefit less fortunate members of the black community. Unwilling to ask for what she could not give, she traveled widely and worked tirelessly on behalf of her race, and on behalf of a more broadly humanitarian vision. As Frances Smith Foster notes, "Harper decided that her personal survival and well-being were inextricably linked with the survival and well-being of the larger society."[3]

The noble characteristics Harper lauds in "Our Greatest Want" vividly animate Janette Alston, the heroine of her short story "The Two Offers," which also appeared in the *Anglo-African Magazine* in 1859. As Frances Smith Foster and Larose Davis note, the short story "introduced to the American literary canon one of the first professional black female protagonists who was educated, single, and successful."[4] Ann duCille writes of this same protagonist: she "chooses a career as a writer and a vocation as an antislavery activist, not necessarily *instead* of loving a man but *because* of loving herself, her genius, her potential."[5] Indeed, Janette loves herself, cares for the poor, assists the enslaved, and resolves, as Harper puts it, to "kindle the fires of her genius on the altars of universal love and truth."[6]

This chapter explores and expands on the recurring theme of love in "The Two Offers" whose heroine privileges solidarity over individualism and positions service over self-interest. Below, it examines Janette's formative moments: losing suffering family members to death, parting with her beloved, and committing herself to antiracist activism. Drawing on affect theory to analyze suffering, examining love-driven politics,[7] and positing the value of sentiment, this chapter argues for the political implications of intrapersonal and interpersonal relations rooted in love. Specifically, it builds on bell hooks's observation that "[t]o truly love we must learn to mix various ingredients—care, affection, recognition, respect, commitment, and trust, as well as honest and open communication,"[8] and configures love as an antiracist principle with the power to engender alternative ways of being-in-the-world. That is, it is both a mode of resistance and an agent of positive and non-coercive social change.

Resonating with towering figures like civil rights activist Dr. Martin L. King, Jr., essayist and novelist James Baldwin, and playwright Lorraine Hansberry, hooks's *Salvation: Black People and Love* posits love as integral to social movements striving to eradicate racism, sexism, classism, and imperialism. Specifically, she argues that "[w]e cannot effectively resist domination if our efforts to create meaningful, lasting personal and social change are not grounded in a love ethic."[9] Theorizing love's transformative power, hooks further asserts, "all spheres of American life—politics, religion, the workplace, domestic households, intimate relations—should and could have as their foundation a love ethic."[10] Evoking Dr. King's love inspired "beloved community," Baldwin's "love letter" to his fourteen-year-old nephew facing ugly race hatred, and Mama's injunction in Hansberry's *Raisin* that "there is always something left to love" in family members who disappoint us,[11] hooks highlights the history of anti-racist love in black social movements and literature, illuminating its relevance in twenty-first-century struggles. Striking a prophetic note, she urges readers to "return" to love, which she defines as "care, respect, knowledge, and responsibility."[12] Moving beyond narrow individualism privileging the self, love requires a broader view, a wider awareness of others' lived experiences and a willingness to engage them.

Elaborating and expanding upon hooks's definition of love, Kelly Oliver argues that "Love is the ethical agency that motivates a move toward others, across differences. Love motivates a move beyond self-interested political action, which is a necessary move beyond domination."[13] Developing an interest in persons beyond the self requires sustained, directed attention, as well as actions that honor and respect others. But this attitude becomes possible, writes Oliver, when we look with a "loving eye" that is "a critical eye in the sense that it is necessary, crucial for establishing and nourishing relationships across difference."[14] Ever vigilant, the "loving eye is always on the lookout for the blind spots that close off the possibility of response-ability and openness to others and difference."[15] Such a love recognizes the fundamental humanity bridging difference, and works to eliminate blind spots—what hooks would describe as "continued allegiance to systems of domination—imperialism, sexism, racism, [and] classism."[16] Love for others manifests itself in three forms in this chapter: familial, romantic, and neighborly. In these contexts I define love as mercy, compassion, and care (for the self and others); resonating with hooks's theory, my analysis posits love as an attitude *and* a choice, as the very "action we take on behalf of our own or another's spiritual growth."[17]

Compassion resonates as a key theme in "The Two Offers" and as a touchstone in Harper's extraordinary life. Born Frances Ellen Watkins to free black parents in Maryland in 1825, Harper was orphaned at the age of three.[18] Scholars suggest a relative cared for Harper, who attended and excelled at her uncle Reverend William Watkins's Academy for Negro Youth, a respected institution that offered a rigorous curriculum focusing on Greek, Latin, elocution, and biblical studies.[19] It also emphasized "Christian service" and "political leadership," the very skills and values that Harper would cultivate and exemplify throughout her politically active life.[20] Still in her teens, Harper moved to Baltimore, where she worked as a domestic. In 1845, she published *Forest Leaves*, a collection of poems routinely listed in biographical sketches of Harper but recently discovered.[21] Around 1850, she was hired to teach at Union Seminary, and in 1852 she relocated to Pennsylvania where she continued teaching. But her life changed dramatically in 1853, when Maryland passed a law making free blacks eligible to be sold as slaves. Soon thereafter, Harper devoted herself full-time to the abolitionist cause.[22]

She would go on to write across genres and serve her community variously as a poet, temperance advocate, teacher, fiction writer, and antislavery lecturer. In 1853 she published a book of poetry, *Eliza Harris*, and in 1854 she published another book, *Poems on Miscellaneous Subjects*. In that same year, the Maine Anti-Slavery Society hired Harper, who promoted the anti-slavery cause throughout northeastern states and in Canada.

Harper married widower Fenton Harper in 1860 and moved to Ohio, where she gave birth to one child and cared for her husband's three children, while continuing to publish and give occasional lectures during the next four years.[23] When Fenton Harper died in 1864, Harper resumed lecturing for the antislavery cause. After the Civil War ended, she taught and lectured throughout the South. Harper published four collections of poetry between 1869 and 1872, and published a serialized novel, *Minnie's Sacrifice,* in 1869. Two additional short novels would follow, *Sowing and*

Reaping: A Temperance Story (1876) and *Trial and Triumph* (1888–1889), and in 1892, she published *Iola Leroy, or Shadows Uplifted*, her only full-length and most popular novel. As I argue in *Courting Communities* (2006), *Iola Leroy* makes a key contribution to interrogations of nationalism as the novel speaks within and against this political philosophy in important ways. Harper, like Maria W. Stewart, Anna Julia Cooper, and Mary Ann Shadd Cary, drew selectively on nationalist themes such as self-help and racial uplift to "imagine community" through textual production.[24] After *Iola Leroy*, Harper published several essays and collections of poetry, while participating in a range of political organizations, including the Women's Christian Temperance Union and the National Association of Colored Women.

As noted above, Harper published "The Two Offers," believed to be one of the first short stories by an African American woman, in the *Anglo-African Magazine*, a periodical founded in New York City by black journalist Thomas Hamilton in 1859. In the first issue of the magazine's "Apology," Hamilton laments that "[t]he wealth, the intellect, the Legislation, . . . the pulpit, and the science of America, have concentrated on no one point so heartily as in the endeavor to write down the negro as something less than a man."[25] Against institutional forces mobilizing antiblack discourse to justify slavery and racial oppression, Hamilton offered African Americans a textual space to represent themselves as free agents capable of thinking for themselves and documenting their own lives. Toward this end, his Apology declares that "[a]ll articles in the Magazine, not otherwise designated, will be the products of the pens of colored men and women, from whom we earnestly solicit contributions."[26] Harper's writings, which humanize African Americans, coincide with Hamilton's goals to represent blacks with dignity and to detail the racist conditions shaping daily their daily lives. As Melba Joyce Boyd asserts, Harper often "enlists arguments to deconstruct social inequalities, historical distortions, and vicious lies to confront the status quo."[27] Indeed, Harper achieves these goals in her body of work and in "The Two Offers," specifically, she highlights social concerns such as slavery, poverty, women's rights, and temperance in a sentimental framework.

"The Two Offers" appeared in two installments in September and October 1859. Briefly summarized, the story opens with an exchange between fair-skinned cousins, Janette and Laura, the latter of whom must decide which of two marriage proposals to accept. Despite Janette's sober warning that Laura marry based on an "affinity of souls," Laura instead marries a "vain and superficial man" susceptible to alcoholism and "midnight haunts."[28] While the birth of their beautiful baby temporarily halts his irresponsible behavior, the child is soon visited by the "angel of death" and Laura's husband resumes drinking. Grieving her child's premature death and husband's eventual desertion, Laura—a sad and wearied woman—dies from a broken heart. Janette, however, remains single, self-fulfilled, and secure in her conviction that it is better to be "an old maid who accepts her earthly mission as a gift from God," rather than a woman bound "in an ill-assorted marriage."[29] Her mission to love and serve the poor, which crystallizes after Laura dies, proves subversive, as personal grief and neighborly concern produce a politically informed sensibility.

Pivotal scholars such as Frances Smith Foster (1990), Melba Joyce Boyd (1994), Hazel V. Carby (1987), Carla Peterson (1995), and others focus collectively on Harper's vast cultural production including her poems, essays, speeches, and fiction. Rather than examine the breadth of Harper's accomplishments, however, this chapter focuses solely on the short story that has received limited critical attention.

Much of the small but vibrant body of scholarship addressing "The Two Offers" analyzes the racial ambiguity of Harper's characters, as well as her treatment of restrictive female gender roles, middle-class values, and the ruinous effects of intemperance on domesticity. William J. Scheick, for example, contends that Laura and Janette are "white women" and that a "recognition of mutual bondage apparently informs Janette's final identification with the African-American slave."[30] Conversely, Carby argues the story was "addressed to both white and black audiences of both sexes,"[31] while Carla Peterson notes "the narrator refuses to give the reader a detailed physical description of her heroine."[32] By the story's end, however, "Janette . . . merges not only with Watkins Harper but with the narrator whose fictional self depends on Watkins Harper's historical existence." In effect, "the narrator chooses Janette" over Laura as "a model for black women."[33]

Elaborating on racial ambiguity in "The Two Offers," Deborah J. Rosenthal suggests that Harper wrote the story "specifically for black readers" who "probably did not find the deracialized discourse curious, but instead assumed Harper's characters to be black."[34] In addition, writes Rosenthal, "the racial ambiguity" in the story, "which suggests that characters who could be black lead lives indistinguishable from those of white Americans, indicates that middle-class respectability is a right in itself."[35] Shelley Block disagrees, suggesting "that instead of arguing for the collusion of black and middle-class values, 'The Two Offers,' in the context of the *Anglo-African*, declaims capitalistic middle-class values, utilizing temperance as a backdrop for a rhetoric of social revolution to replace white bourgeois values."[36] Carolyn Sorisio argues Harper's temperance writings often call attention to "the intemperate body, often either deracializing that body or hinting that it may be Caucasian,"[37] while DoVeannna Fulton extends this debate, suggesting that "[ra]cial indeterminacy opens the text to multiple and varied engagements by different reading communities" and allows Harper to proffer a radical integrationist vision of America in which communities, though class stratified, are peopled by individuals whose race is insignificant to the context of the narrative."[38] Fulton further details Harper's participation in and critique of racially discriminatory practices in the Women's Christian Temperance Union, an organization founded by women in 1874 to promote abstinence from alcohol.[39]

A number of key works on "The Two Offers" also explore how Harper subversively situates her short story within and against the American sentimental literary tradition. Sentimental literature, which I discuss at length in chapter 2, has long been criticized as subliterary, sensational, and detached from harsh sociopolitical realities. In *Sentimental Designs*, Jane Tompkins reevaluates what she calls the "specifically female novelistic tradition," which had "at least since the middle of the nineteenth century" been "rigorously excluded from the ranks of 'serious' literary works."[40] She aims her critique primarily at the "male-dominated scholarly tradition" whose "critics have taught generations of students to equate popularity with debasement, emotionality with ineffectiveness, religiosity with fakery, domesticity with triviality, and all of these, implicitly, with womanly inferiority."[41] In her effort to understand these texts, Tompkins argues that we must situate them in their historical contexts, understand "the cultural realities that made these novels meaningful," and consider "the specific problems to which they were addressed.[42] Namely, these novels represent a "tradition of evangelical piety and moral commitment" that "in certain cases . . . offe[r] a critique of American society."[43] Tompkins cites the antislavery novel *Uncle Tom's Cabin* as a prime example of a sentimental text functioning as a "political enterprise, halfway between sermon and social theory, that both codifies and attempts to mold the values of its time."[44]

Since the publication of *Sentimental Designs,* a proliferation of progressive readings have explored the political implications of the form. According to Glenn Hendler, "During the 1980s and 1990s, one tendency in the analysis of nineteenth-century American literature and culture has been what Eve Sedgwick calls 'a project . . . of rehabilitating the sentimental' from critical neglect and knee-jerk denigration."[45] An important part of this project of literary "rehabilitation," Claudia Tate's *Domestic Allegories of Political Desire* focuses on black women's subjectivity and "stories about racial justice and female autonomy,"[46] while Joanne Dobson employs a culturally situated and "traditionally literary approach" to sentimental writing in "Reclaiming Sentimental Literature."[47]

Scholarship focusing specifically on "The Two Offers" suggests Harper reinforces and rebels against sentimental literary conventions. Peterson, for example, describes the normative link between temperance and sentimentality:

> [i]n accordance with sentimental ideology, temperance stories posit a beneficent feminine domestic sphere ruled by pure moral values that stands in opposition to the male public sphere whose corrupt values

are symbolized by the spaces of the saloon, the gambling house, and the brothel. In emphasizing the isolation, dependence, and physical vulnerability, and the social immobility of married women, such stories underscore the extent to which they are victims of oppression.[48]

Reinforcing this framework, Laura becomes the ultimate victim of her drunken husband. On the other hand, Janette boldly defies stereotypical representations of the nineteenth-century "true woman" who is too fragile to engage in the hurly-burly of the public sphere. As Barbara Welter's groundbreaking essay notes, between 1820 and 1860, dominant culture represented true women as white, pious, pure, submissive, and primarily invested in domestic affairs.[49] Marriage was considered the ideal site for women to engage in domestic affairs but singleness was preferable to an unhappy and unhealthy marriage.[50] Harper indeed embraces the cult of true womanhood by celebrating the power of the loving mother in the home, but she also subverts it by constructing a "self-reliant" heroine committed to transgressive social activism.[51] Peterson similarly asserts that Harper "appropriated sentimental ideology and its construction of the private-public dichotomy to critique it and celebrate instead the single woman who, like herself, insists on seizing the public sphere as her field of action."[52] DuCille similarly notes that Harper engages in "rewriting, if not completely debunking, the notions and limitations of the ideology of true womanhood,"[53] while Boyd suggests the story reveals "her advocacy of women's independent spirit."[54]

Building on this insightful body of scholarship detailing Harper's revision of the sentimental tradition, I focus on affective distress in Harper's story and explore Janette's trajectory from suffering to loving public service. I also draw on psychologist Silvan Tomkins's theory of affect to analyze how Janette engages the oppressed, concluding that Harper employs scenes of distress to generate readers' social action.[55] Describing the affect of distress, Tomkins writes that its "major sources" can "arise from the body, its pains and illnesses, from work and its problems, and from the vicissitudes of interpersonal relationships. The environment is constantly also creating new disturbances and challenges which create distress."[56] He agrees with Darwin that "crying expresses suffering 'both bodily pain and mental distress,'" yet significantly notes that one of the "biological function[s] of crying" is "to motivate both the self and others to do something to reduce the crying response."[57] While distress may or may not invoke tears, Tomkins notes this affect can call forth a response from onlookers. Specifically, he writes that "[d]istress is not a toxic crippling affect" but rather it "promotes remedial strategies which can attack the sources of distress."[58] Moreover, Tomkins claims, "No one has to urge distress upon anyone who becomes aware that a beloved is suffering."[59] Underscoring the relational nature of affects, Tomkins suggests that one who cares for another readily sees and strives to alleviate the loved one's distress. An attentive watchfulness compels such a person to ease the beloved's pain. But in the absence of positive affect, a relation of identification must be developed to motivate action on behalf of the suffering.[60]

Using Tomkins's framework, I suggest that Harper "motivates" readers to identify with her distressed characters and engage in social activism. Specifically the story evokes readers' sympathy for and sociopolitical response to the oppressed by modeling compassionate activism in "The Two Offers." Given the story's publication in the *Anglo-African Magazine*, a periodical produced by black authors specifically for a black readership, I read Janette and Laura as African American characters who represent conflicting worldviews within the black middle-class.

A FAMILY AFFAIR

A veritable model for readers, Janette *moves toward* distressed members of her family, conscientiously caring for her ailing mother and cousin, a point made forcefully in the scenes describing Janette's relationship with her widowed mother. After Janette's father dies, she "watched over her [mother] with untiring devotion" as she endured "pitiless pelting storms of adversity."[61] By "watching over," Janette bears witness to her mother's suffering, acknowledges her distress, and finally "close[s] her eyes in death."[62] Visiting the sick and burying the dead, designated as "works of mercy" in theological frameworks, require "attentiveness and sensitivity to the concrete needs we encounter."[63] In the language of Tomkins's affect theory, which emphasizes physical reactions to stimuli, the mother's distress arises "from the body, its pains and illnesses" and also from the "new disturbances" developing after her husband's death.[64] Namely, the husband died "in an embarrassed state" and so his widow "wrestled with want till her toil-worn hands became too feeble to hold the shattered chords [sic] of existence."[65] Financial hardships burden the mother and hasten her physical decline. As Tomkins notes, "economic depressions" can "subject children, adolescents, and adults alike to severe distress over which they can exercise little control."[66] Such is the case with Janette, who cannot alleviate her mother's distress. This instructive scene works on at least three levels, evoking sympathy for the dying mother, problematizing married women in the domestic sphere who are "unacquainted with [their husbands'] business affairs," and critiquing the "hungry creditors" who take advantage of such women.[67] Moreover, this critical passage depicts Janette as the model of compassion worthy of readers' emulation. In this and subsequent moments of crisis, Janette draws near to those who suffer and embarks on a life of service to aid those in need. Notably, after caring for her mother, Janette looks after her cousin Laura, whose marital woes produce a "deep yearning for home sympathy."[68]

Hendler asserts that in the eighteenth and nineteenth centuries, sympathy was much like compassion in that "what one must feel is the suffering of others."[69] Sympathy, he elaborates, is "an emotional response to reading or seeing an expression of another's feelings. It is thus at its core an act of identification. To feel compassion, as opposed to mere pity, one must be able to imagine oneself, at least to some extent, in another's position."[70] Janette is among the sympathetic family members who connect imaginatively with Laura, feel for the sorrowful woman, and "for [Laura's] sake . . . wished [her husband's] coming."[71] In a dual move, Harper records Janette's sympathetic response and depicts Laura—the victim of her drunken husband—as worthy of readers' sympathy. Desertion and "deat[h] of a love object" are the source of Laura's distress and the conditions over which she is powerless.[72] Represented as weak and vulnerable, her character invites tears and even outrage for the thoughtless drunk who casts her aside.

The emotional scene describing Janette's connection to Laura also encourages reader identification with Janette, who strives in vain to alleviate Laura's suffering. This identification is accomplished, in part, by the fact that Janette is among the "sad watchers by that dying bed" in whose eyes "tears gathered."[73] For the second time in the story, she extends compassion to a dying loved one and grieves her impending loss, and she does so in a manner that is entirely selfless, her emotions manifesting her regard for a suffering person. In his analysis of affect, Tomkins states that "the presence of distress indicates a potential for remedial action."[74] While Janette willingly attends to Laura's distress, she is unable to relieve her pain. In this helpless and tearful state, Janette evokes sympathy because she is vulnerable and unable to improve her cousin's condition. Again represented as a loving individual turning toward rather than away from pain, Janette models compassion, which Harper also works to cultivate in her readers.

LOVING IN PUBLIC

Following earnestly the Bible's teachings on neighborly love, Janette tends to family and community members alike. More specifically, she determines at Laura's deathbed "more earnestly than ever to make the world better by her example,"[75] and she ministers to others to achieve this goal. In the Bible, Jesus identifies the "greatest commandment" as love of God and love of neighbor (Mark 12:29–31; Matt. 22:34–40; Luke 10:25–28), and includes among the "works of love" feeding the hungry (Matt. 25:35–39). Grounded in this tradition, Janette recognizes the slave as her neighbor by "extend[ing]" herself on his behalf, to use hooks's language of service and love.[76] More specifically, "In [Janette], the downtrodden slave found an earnest advocate; the flying fugitive remembered her kindness as he stepped cautiously through our Republic, to gain his freedom in a monarchal land."[77] Words like "down-trodden" and "flying" emphasize the slave's desperate condition and his urgent need for help. That he steps "cautiously" reminds readers that America, for the slave, is treacherous ground to be traversed en route to freedom. A crusader for justice, Janette apparently bestows personal "kindness" upon fugitives seeking liberty and wages war against slavery with her pen. Expressing solidarity with the slave, she "willingly espouse[s] an unpopular cause" and honors the dignity of the socially denigrated slave.[78]

Venturing beyond the comforts of middle-class existence, Janette also centers the marginalized poor in her social activist efforts.[79] Hooks writes that "to be in the margin is to be part of the whole but outside of the main body" and theorizes about the "knowledge and awareness of the lives of women and men who live on the margin."[80] Janette exists with the poor on the margin due to sex and race inequality, but she has class privilege relative to the black poor. Specifically, the "achievements of her genius had won her a position in the literary world" and "with her fame came a competence of worldly means, which gave her leisure for improvement."[81] Though she is financially secure and well educated, Janette's lived experience as a gendered and racialized subject provides access to "hidden knowledge" acquired in the margin. She knows that sex and race impede access to freedom and equality, and works to address these inequalities. Using her privilege to assist rather than oppress, Janette reaches across class lines to engage the needy and as such, "the poor called her blessed, as she broke her bread to the pale lips of hunger."[82] Sharing her resources and herself, Janette embraces loving-kindness as a core social value.

Consciously defying the "coupling convention,"[83] Janette instead enters into a circuit of neighborly love. Notably, Janette is unmarried yet she resists "pining at her loneliness and isolation" as "the world was full of warm, loving hearts, and her own beat in unison with them."[84] These simultaneous and harmonious heartbeats in Janette's social "world" illustrate her fundamental relation to community. As Tess Chakkalakal observes,

> The story introduces readers to the novel idea, personified by Janette Alston, "that true happiness consists not so much in the fruition of our wishes as in the regulation of desires and the full development and right culture of our whole natures." Read in this way, marriage is only a part of the story; the real story lies in Janette herself, who leads a good and productive life without the support of a husband.[85]

"The Two Offers" thus depicts a single woman who communes with "loving hearts" in her community and finds happiness without a husband. As Harper puts it, Janette was not "always sentimentally sighing for something to love, objects of affection were all around her, and the world was not so wealthy in love that it had no use for her's" [*sic*].[86] Harper's characterization conjoins "wealthy" with "love" to redefine riches, such that Janette enriches the world—not with gold—but with loving kindness and compassion. That she has "a higher and better object in all her writings than the acquisition of gold" allows Harper to position this costly metal as subordinate to the priceless practices of loving one's neighbor and crusading for justice."[87]

ORIGIN STORIES

Janette's spiritual and communal values contrast sharply with the materialism perverting the childhood homes and adult lives of Laura and her husband. The home of Janette's youth was "rich only in goodness and affection," and she watched as her mother was "sheltered in the warm clasp of [her father's] loving arms."[88] Learning from her parents' example and subsequent personal suffering, Janette becomes a compassionate and socially responsible human being. On the other hand, Laura's "rich and indulgent parents . . . had spared no pains to make her an accomplished lady."[89] Privileging material desires over spiritual values, her parents raised an appearance-oriented "lady," unable to read the "true character" of the man she "blindly loved."[90] Accordingly, she died heartbroken and abandoned. Unfortunately, her husband's upbringing was no better:

> In early life, home had been to him a place of ceilings and walls, not a true home, built upon goodness, love, and truth. . . . His father had been too much engrossed in making money, and his mother in spending it, striving to maintain a fashionable position in society. . . . His mother put beautiful robes upon his body, but left ugly scars upon his soul; she pampered his appetite, but starved his spirit.[91]

Tracing the husband's intemperate lifestyle to parental selfishness, greed, and pride, Harper places responsibility on parents generally, and mothers specifically, to shape their children's inner life. Reinforcing in this context traditional domestic values, the story privileges women's role in the home such that "[e]very mother should be a true poet capable of writing on the soul of childhood the harmony of love and truth, and teaching it how to produce the grandest of all poems—the poetry of a true and noble life."[92] That is, ideal mothers should be teacher-artists who expose their children to spiritual values and principles. But more, mothers should be "poets" who use and teach their children the power of language. I agree with Block that Harper "depicts middle class, bourgeoisie culture as being equally detrimental to male and female members of black society," and elaborate on her claim that "rejecting intemperance requires the rejection of middle-class white materialism and the embracing of black communal values, including abolition."[93] Compassionate, loving regard for the distressed and oppressed ranks high among these communal values that profoundly shape Janette's private and public life.

Harper explores sympathy and service in other ways as well. Importantly, Janette's personal suffering renders her sympathetic to readers and further prepares her to serve others. In the first section of the story, for example, readers glimpse into Janette's past when she had loved "wildly, passionately." The "painful separation" that followed, however, left her "spirit-broken." Although she "tried to break the chain of sad associations that bound her to the mournful past," she faltered and endured agony of heartbreak.[94] Clearly, Janette has an experiential understanding of suffering that makes her worthy of sympathy and positions her to empathize with others in distress.

Death imagery illustrates the healing process forcing Janette to dig "the sepulcher of her happiness, and then a new-made grave" so that she can lay her sorrow to rest. Unexpectedly, while suffering and "pressing back the bitter sobs from her almost breaking heart," Janette undergoes a kind of literary rebirth as "her genius gathered strength from suffering."[95] Subsequently, "[m]en hailed her as one of earth's strangely gifted children" but she continued lamenting her loss and felt "a deep yearning for sympathy and heart support."[96] Affect theorist Tompkins writes: "[t]he general biological function of crying is . . . to communicate to the organism itself and to others that all is not well" and also "to motivate both the self and others to do something to reduce the crying response."[97] Since Janette hides her tears (signifying distress) from others by "pressing back the bitter sobs," onlookers remain unaware of her pain and unable to alleviate her suffering. Taking her own "remedial strategies,"[98] Janette steels herself to meet life's "solemn responsibilities."[99] This critical period of anguish renders Janette worthy of reader sympathy as she is a good person who meets with undeserved yet relatable human adversity. Quite remarkably, her trials prepare her to serve others such that, upon recovering, her "looks and tones are full of sympathy and love."[100] Literally changed, Janette's emotional pain has affected her very being and shaped her disposition, equipping her to feel deeply for and gaze with a "loving eye" upon her fellow human beings.

"The Two Offers" calls upon middle-class readers to recognize and exercise their capacity for sympathy. As Janette sympathetically engages society's most disadvantaged members, "The Two Offers" encourages black middle-class readers to sympathize with Janette's struggles *and* emulate her social activism. The narrative early invites sympathy for Janette, whose parents die too soon, leaving her to fend for herself in an unpredictable world. The image of a young woman facing struggles alone is sufficient to bring tears and corresponds to nineteenth-century sentimental conventions. But the evocation of a tearful reader does not reduce the story to pure sentimentality. Rather, sentimentality is used as a vehicle for directing the reader toward more substantive concerns. As Baym notes in her study of middle-class white women's novels from 1820–1870, "[t]hese novels . . . all tell about a young woman who has lost the emotional and financial support of her legal guardians . . . who nevertheless goes on to make her own way in the world."[101] "The Two Offers" is a short story but it repeats this trajectory of women's novels with signal revisions, such as featuring an African American woman in a middle-class context. Janette loses her parents at an early age and she consequently ventures into the "restless world" (which was thought to be no place for a young woman), where she "supports herself by her own exertions."[102] In addition, her heartbreak is rendered in highly emotional language to call forth readers' affective response: at one juncture, her heart "was throbbing with a wild and fearful unrest" as she endured "her almost breaking heart."[103]

According to Peterson, Harper "appropriated the sentimental discourse that had entered and permeated white women's culture by way of the eighteenth-century European cult of sensibility . . . that would excite readers' compassion and move them not to emotional consumption but to productive action."[104] I would suggest Janette's emotionalism serves to incite sympathy, while her determination to persevere and help others encourages "productive action." Put another way, the narrative encourages readers to identify with Janette's pain *and* to admire her for overcoming it. Despite her "shattered spirit," for example, Janette turns back to "life's duties" with "calmness and strength."[105] She earns the narrator's admiration for her "lovely spirit" and recognition as "her life was like a beautiful story."[106] With these favorable observations, the narrator renders unqualified approval of Janette and presents her as an example for readers to follow. That Janette's capacity to love has been increased rather than diminished by loss is instructive and potentially inspiring. While the texts Baym examines "hoped to guide . . . readers' thinking about choice of mate and married life," and to "delineate the type of women who could construct [the middle-class household as] a base and operate productively from it,"[107] Harper complicates this tradition by foregrounding race and an unmarried black woman who finds spiritual fulfillment in community service.

LOVING COMMUNITY

Read through a racial lens, Janette's solidarity with the black community illustrates the value of racial uplift activism. Here I depart from Scheick, who finds Janette's "decision to join the antislavery cause . . . sudden and emphatically elliptical."[108] For Scheick, "nothing in the story, read superficially, seems to prepare for it, especially since no previous comment refers to the plight of African-American slave."[109] However, a consideration of Harper's intended audience and her choice of publication venue makes possible alternative readings. Like Foster and Rosenthal, I make a case for reading Janette as black, and also suggest she performs the very social work that Harper endorses in "Our Greatest Want." Historians James and Lois Horton write that "[a]lthough most blacks welcomed the assistance of progressive white reformers, they believed that by working together in black groups they could play an important part in the elevation of the race and the abolition of slavery."[110] Invested in community self-determination, Harper involved herself in numerous racial uplift projects to improve the material conditions of African Americans. Similarly, in "The Two Offers" Janette crosses the gap of economic privilege to identify with the oppressed—much like Iola, the mulatta heroine in Harper's full-length postbellum novel, *Iola Leroy* (1892). While Harper's novel differs dramatically from the short story in form and content, the works share a depiction of middle-class, fair skinned protagonists who align with and serve the black poor. Neither of Harper's texts posits love as a utopian response to eliminate racism and inequality, but the heroines' subversive acts affirm the worth and dignity of African Americans in an antiblack society.

The black female characters in *Politics and Affect* who love themselves and embrace their community necessarily resist oppressive racist and sexist ideologies. But they do so by using specific political strategies. Harper offers an astute commentary on black women living under the oppressive conditions of white supremacy, considering, among other things, how racism impacts self-worth. Specifying black women's unique sociopolitical condition, historian Deborah Gray White states,

> For antebellum black women . . . sexism was but one of three constraints. Most were slaves. . . . They were slaves because they were black, and even more than sex, color was a mark of degradation, so much so that in most Southern states one's dark complexion was *prima facie* evidence that one was a slave. Black in a white society, slave in a free society, woman in a society ruled by men, female slaves had the least formal power and were the most vulnerable group of antebellum Americans.[111]

White describes the conditions facing enslaved black women, whom I discuss in chapter 2, and also characterizes the racial and sexual discrimination impacting Janette's experience as a free black woman. While Janette is fair-skinned and does not overtly reference her race in the narrative, she is arguably legally "black" and embedded in a racist society.

Clearly rejecting white supremacist values rendering blackness unlovable, and countering the conclusion that color was "a mark of degradation," Janette recognizes her worth as a black woman writer and a child of God. Earlier I quoted duCille, who observes that Janette "chooses a career as a writer and a vocation as an antislavery activist, not necessarily *instead* of loving a man but *because* of loving herself, her genius, her potential."[112] Indeed, Janette refuses to internalize antiblack ideologies and instead "accepts her earthly mission as a gift from God," confidently embarking on "a high and holy mission on the battle-field of existence."[113] In turn, her mission to serve the antislavery cause affirms black humanity, generally, and resists racialized discourses dehumanizing and demeaning her community.

By making her main character both black and a woman living under white supremacy, Harper offers philosophical reflections on identity, self worth, and sympathetic understanding. Dwelling at the intersection of race and sex, Janette reinforces the worth of the single black woman. Significantly, she rejects Laura's patriarchal premise that being an "old maid" is "not to be thought of,"[114] and lives a fulfilled life without a mate. Through her own achievements, Janette represents black women's capacity to surpass race and gender stereotypes, and their potential to make valuable contributions to community. In *Race Matters*, Cornel West writes that "[s]elf-love and love of others are both modes toward increasing self-valuation and encouraging political resistance in one's community."[115] In a similar fashion, Janette's demonstrable regard for self and other inspires her to engage and aid her community.

Janette's communal investments reconfigure the liberal individual model of the autonomous subject by privileging interpersonal obligations over individualism. As we've seen, Janette cares lovingly for her ailing relatives but her compassion extends beyond familial borders. Indeed, after her cousin dies, Janette "resolved more earnestly than ever to make the world better by her example, gladder by her presence."[116] This critical turning point marks Janette's expansion from loving in the privacy of domesticity to "loving out loud" in public.[117] Directing her energy toward the broader African American community, Janette participates in the anti-slavery cause by "kindl[ing] the fires of her genius on the altars of universal love."[118] Eschewing individualism and embarking on a love-driven politics in a social setting, Janette pens abolitionist poems to help turn public sentiment against slavery.

Moreover, Harper's depiction of social engagement necessarily enlarges narrow conceptions of self rooted in liberal individual subjectivity. I agree with Boyd that "The Two Offers" endorses women's "independent spirit," and Hildegard Hoeller who further claims, "Harper develops a sense of 'self-reliance' that carries much of the original meaning of the term in Emerson's essay but that also includes sympathy for others, solidarity among oppressed groups, and a sense of race and gender identity."[119] Extending these readings of Janette's subjectivity to their philosophical underpinnings, I suggest that Harper challenges the liberal individual subject that Susan Hekman describes as "autonomous or 'unencumbered,'"[120] and rejects "the unified, apparently ungendered individual of liberalism [that] masks structures of male privilege and domination."[121] Harper's story also disrupts what Margaret McLaren describes as the "rationality that has historically excluded women" and its "abstraction from the concrete, material world, both in terms of the erasure of the body and the neglect of the social relationships and institutions on which every subject depends"[122]

Janette's lived experience as a black woman connected to community contradicts liberalism's universalist and patriarchal assumptions. Specifically, Harper depicts Janette in the text as an intellectual black woman capable of rational thinking and deep feeling.[123] And by the story's end, as Peterson argues, Janette "merges" with the narrator,[124] who wisely calls for female education that develops both woman's emotions and "all the faculties of the human soul."[125] The call for a holistic model of education recognizes the specific social barriers denying women as a group (and black women to a greater extent) equal access to education. Honing in on the specificity of black women's experiences, Harper's story envisions a comprehensive model of education for those who must have faced the myriad obstacles Jacqueline Jones Royster enumerates:

> Further complicating women's place in higher education for African American women were the stereotypes about character that continued to plague them because of their roles as "breeders" and rape victims during slavery and because of the images of them as being licentious, amoral, and animalistic. After the Civil War, as well as before, African American women were not just restricted in terms of sphere, as in the case of white women, they also remained degraded and devalued.[126]

The black women Royster describes, free and enslaved, necessarily refuted antiblack stereotypes reducing them to subhuman beings and limiting their access to full citizenship rights. Speaking to these same concerns, "The Two Offers" intervenes in racist and sexist discourses, constructing an affirming image of a black woman gifted with a "double portion of intellect,"[127] and the capacity to regulate her desires.[128] As African Americans, Janette and her community confront structural oppressions rendering moot the fantasy of liberal autonomy.

Continuing the work Harper and other activists began in the antebellum period, in 1896 a Miss Margaret Black adds her voice to the struggle in the "Women's Column" of *The Afro-American* newspaper:

> When it is considered what beneficial things the women have wrought in the world, what they have done in science, art and literature. In religion and politics, even through debarred from the higher education of the great schools, it can readily be believed that if the bars were removed the achievements of women in all paths which they could tread with dignity would be equal to those of men.[129]

Miss Black recognizes the considerable gains African American women have made despite racial discrimination and challenges the structures preventing them from competing as men's equals.

Aware that women's subordinate condition is not "natural" but socially produced, she agitates for change. Her efforts join the chorus of Harper, Julia Collins, Anna Julia Cooper, and others from the antebellum to the post-Emancipation period who would fundamentally reclaim black women's subjectivity from their oppressors and rewrite black women as creative, thinking, feeling, agents of change.

In "Our Greatest Want," Harper notes the power of "[l]eading ideas" that "impress themselves upon communities and countries," weaving themselves into the "mental and moral life" of the masses.[130] Writing against the racism, selfishness, and greed characterizing her culture, Harper calls for a shift toward spiritual values and endorses the "glorious idea of human brotherhood."[131] Carrying these themes forward in fiction, and exploring key philosophical questions about what it means to occupy the subject position of a black woman, writer, and activist in the nineteenth century, Harper selects a heroine who wages a discursive war against slavery, assists the fugitives in flight, and tenderly loves her neighbor within and beyond the private sphere. Janette's social activism strikes a spiritual note, for "[i]n blessing others she made a life and benediction."[132] In other words, love-driven activism constitutes for Janette a vocation, making her a blessing unto others. A model to readers, Janette resists liberal individualism and stretches beyond class boundaries to touch and serve those who suffer in the margins. Configuring an expansive way of being-in-the-world, "The Two Offers" depicts love—not merely as a romantic emotion to enjoy in private, but as a practical politics offered and lived in the world.

NOTES

1. Frances Harper, "Our Greatest Want" in *The Norton Anthology of African American Literature,* eds. Henry Louis Gates, Jr., and Valerie A. Smith et al., vol. 1., third edition (New York: W. W. Norton, 2014), 467.

2. Harper, "Our Greatest Want," 468.

3. Frances Smith Foster, *A Brighter Coming Day: A Frances Ellen Watkins Harper Reader,* ed. Frances Smith Foster (New York: The Feminist Press, 1990), 3.

4. Frances Smith Foster and Larose Davis, "Early African American Women's Literature" in *The Cambridge Companion to African American Women's Literature,* eds. Angelyn K. Mitchell and Danille K. Taylor (New York: Cambridge University Press, 2009), 22.

5. Ann duCille, *The Coupling Convention: Sex, Text, and Tradition in Black Women's Fiction* (New York: Oxford University Press, 1993), 64, original emphasis.

6. Frances Harper, "The Two Offers," in *The Norton Anthology of African American Literature,* eds. Henry Louis Gates, Jr., and Valerie A. Smith et al., vol. 1., third edition (New York: W. W. Norton, 2014), 466.

7. I borrow the phrase "love-driven politics" from a series of conversations initiated by Drs. David Kim and George Lipsitz at an informal scholarly gathering at the Union Theological Seminary in New York on March 28, 2015.

8. bell hooks, *All About Love: New Visions* (New York: Perennial, 2000), 5.

9. bell hooks, *Salvation: Black People and Love* (New York: Perennial, 2001), xxiv.

10. hooks, *All About Love*, 87.
11. James Baldwin, *The Fire Next Time* (New York: Vintage International, 1993). Also, see Lorraine Hansberry, *A Raisin in the Sun and The Sign in Sidney Brustein's Window* (New York: Vintage Books, 1995), 145. For a discussion of Mama's loving stance in *A Raisin in the Sun*, see Tricia Rose, "Hansberry's *A Raisin in the Sun* and the 'Illegible' Politics of (Inter)personal Justice," *KALFOU*, 1(2014): 27–60.
12. hooks, *Salvation*, 4–5.
13. Kelly Oliver, *Witnessing: Beyond Recognition* (Minneapolis: University of Minnesota Press, 2001), 218.
14. Oliver, *Witnessing*, 219.
15. Oliver, *Witnessing*, 20.
16. Qtd. In Oliver, *Witnessing*, 218.
17. hooks, *All About Love*, 54.
18. Foster, *A Brighter Coming Day*, 5–6.
19. Foster, *A Brighter Coming Day*, 7.
20. Foster, *A Brighter Coming Day*, 7.
21. See http://common-place.org/book/lost-no-more-recovering-frances-ellen-watkins-harpers-forest-leaves/. Accessed on January 17, 2017.
22. Hazel V. Carby, *Reconstructing Womanhood: The Emergence of the Afro-American Woman Novelist* (New York: Oxford University Press, 1987), 65.
23. This is a brief sketch of Harper's biography, based on "Frances E.W. Harper" in *The Norton Anthology of African American Literature*, 445–48. Also see Foster, introduction, *A Brighter Coming Day*, 3–40.
24. Kathy Glass, *Courting Communities: Black Female Nationalism and "Syncre-Nationalism" in the Nineteenth-Century North* (New York: Routledge, 2006).
25. Thomas Hamilton, *The Anglo-African Magazine: Volume I–1859* (Arno Press, 1968), 1.
26. Hamilton, *The Anglo-African Magazine*, 4.
27. Melba Joyce Boyd, "Introduction: Discarded Legacy" in *Discarded Legacy: Politics and Poetics in the Life of Frances E.W. Harper, 1825–1911* (Detroit: Wayne State University Press, 1994), 18.
28. Harper, "The Two Offers," 460, 464.
29. Harper, "The Two Offers," 460.
30. William Scheick, "Strategic Ellipsis in Harper's 'The Two Offers,'" *Southern Literary Journal*, 23 (1991):15, 17.
31. Carby, *Reconstructing Womanhood*, 72.
32. Peterson, *Doers of the Word*, 172.
33. Peterson, *Doers of the Word*, 173.
34. Debra J. Rosenthal, "Deracialized Discourse: Temperance and Racial Ambiguity in Harper's 'The Two Offers' and *Sowing and Reaping*" in *The Serpent in the Cup: Temperance in American Literature* (Amherst, University of Massachusetts Press), 155.
35. Rosenthal, "Deracialized Discourse," 156.
36. Shelley Block, "A Revolutionary Aim: The Rhetoric of Temperance in the Anglo-African Magazine," *American Periodicals: A Journal of History, Criticism and Bibliography* 12 (2002): 18.
37. Carolyn Sorisio, *Fleshing Out America: Race, Gender, and the Politics of the Body in American Literature, 1833–1879* (Athens: University of Georgia Press, 2002), 82.
38. DoVeanna S. Fulton, "Sowing Seeds in an Untilled Field: Temperance and Race, Indeterminacy and Recovery in Frances E. W. Harper's *Sowing and Reaping*," *Legacy* 24 (2007): 211.
39. Fulton, "Sowing Seeds," 216. Fulton notes that scholars are unclear as to when Harper joined the W.C.T.U but by 1883, she was serving as the Superintendent of Work among Colored People in the North.
40. Jane Tompkins, *Sensational Designs: The Cultural Work of American Fiction, 1790–1860* (New York: Oxford University Press, 1985), xiv.
41. Tompkins, *Sensational Designs*, 123.

42. Tompkins, *Sensational Designs*, xiii.
43. Tompkins, *Sensational Designs*, 123, 124.
44. Tompkins, *Sensational Designs*, 126.
45. Glenn Hendler, *Public Sentiments: Structures of Feeling in Nineteenth-Century American Literature* (Chapel Hill: The University of North Carolina Press, 2001), 7.
46. Claudia Tate, *Domestic Allegories of Political Desire: The Black Heroine's Text at the Turn of the Century* (New York: Oxford University Press, 1992), 107.
47. Joanne Dobson, "Reclaiming Sentimental Literature," *American Literature: A Journal of Literary History, Criticism, and Bibliography*, 69 (1997): 263–88.
48. Carla Peterson, *"Doers of the Word": African-American Women Speakers and Writers in the North, 1830–1880* (New York: Oxford University Press, 1995), 172.
49. Barbara Welter, "The Cult of True Womanhood: 1820–1860," *American Quarterly*, 18 (1966): 151–74.
50. Welter, "The Cult of True Womanhood," 169.
51. Harper, "The Two Offers," 461.
52. Peterson, *Doers of the Word*, 171.
53. duCille, *Coupling Convention*, 64.
54. Boyd, *Discarded Legacy*, 118.
55. Silvan Tomkins, *Shame and Its Sisters: A Silvan Tomkins Reader*, eds. Eve Kosofsky Sedgwick and Adam Frank (Durham: Duke University Press, 1995). Tomkins argues humans are born with nine innate affects motivating behavior and action.
56. Tomkins, *Shame and Its Sisters*, 119.
57. Tomkins, *Shame and Its Sisters*, 109, 111
58. Tomkins, *Shame and Its Sisters*, 119.
59. Tomkins, *Shame and Its Sisters*, 120.
60. Tomkins, *Shame and Its Sisters*, 120.
61. Harper, "The Two Offers," 460.
62. Harper, "The Two Offers," 460.
63. Specifically, the Catholic Church. The Methodist Church similarly recognizes as merciful visiting the sick and tending others' needs. See http://www.umc.org/how-we-serve/the-wesleyan-means-of-grace. See also Cardinal Walter Kasper, *Mercy: The Essence of the Gospel and the Key to Christian Life* (New York: Paulist Press, 2014), 142–43.
64. Tomkins, *Shame and Its Sisters*, 119.
65. Harper, "The Two Offers," 460.
66. Tomkins, *Shame and Its Sisters*, 119.
67. Harper, "The Two Offers," 460.
68. Harper, "The Two Offers," 465.
69. Hendler, *Public Sentiments*, 3.
70. Hendler, *Public Sentiments*, 3.
71. Harper, "The Two Offers," 465.
72. Tomkins, *Shame and Its Sisters*, 119.
73. Harper, "The Two Offers," 465.
74. Tomkins, *Shame and Its Sisters*, 120.
75. Harper, "The Two Offers," 466.
76. hooks, *All About Love*, 217.
77. Harper, "The Two Offers," 466.
78. Harper, "The Two Offers," 466.
79. See bell hooks, *Feminist Theory: From Margin to Center* (New York: Routledge, 2015). Here, hooks discusses black women's position relative to white women in the feminist movement, but I find her metaphor of margins useful in discussing black Americans' status in the nineteenth century.
80. hooks, Preface to the first edition of *Feminist Theory*, xvii, xviii.
81. Harper, "The Two Offers," 461.
82. Harper, "The Two Offers," 466.
83. See duCille, *The Coupling Convention*.
84. Harper, "The Two Offers," 466.

85. Tess Chakkalakal, *Novel Bondage: Slavery, Marriage, and Freedom in Nineteenth-Century America* (Chicago: University of Illinois Press, 2011), 66.

86. Harper, "The Two Offers," 466. Here, Harper uses "sentimentally" in a derogatory sense, implying superfluous emotion, where elsewhere she uses heightened feelings to generate sympathy for her heroines.

87. Harper, "The Two Offers," 466.
88. Harper, "The Two Offers," 460.
89. Harper, "The Two Offers," 460.
90. Harper, "The Two Offers," 462.
91. Harper, "The Two Offers," 463.
92. Harper, "The Two Offers," 463.
93. Block, "A Revolutionary Aim," 19, 22.
94. Harper, "The Two Offers," 461.
95. Harper, "The Two Offers," 461.
96. Harper, "The Two Offers," 461.
97. Tomkins, *Shame and Its Sisters*, 111.
98. Tomkins, *Shame and Its Sisters*, 119
99. Harper, "The Two Offers," 461.
100. Harper, "The Two Offers," 461.

101. Nina Baym, "Introduction to the Second Edition" in *Woman's Fiction: A Guide to Novels by and about Women in America, 1820–70* (Urbana: University of Illinois Press, 1993), ix.

102. Harper, "The Two Offers," 461.
103. Harper, "The Two Offers," 461.
104. Peterson, *Doers of the Word*, 23.
105. Harper, "The Two Offers," 461.
106. Harper, "The Two Offers," 461, 466.
107. Baym, *Woman's Fiction*, xxvii.
108. Scheick, "Strategic Ellipsis in Harper's 'The Two Offers,'" 15.
109. Scheick, "Strategic Ellipsis in Harper's 'The Two Offers,'" 15.

110. James Oliver Horton and Lois E. Horton, *In Hope of Liberty: Culture, Community and Protest among Northern Free Blacks, 1700–1860* (New York: Oxford University Press, 1997), 223.

111. Deborah Gray White, *Ar'n't I a Woman?: Female Slaves in the Plantation South* (New York: W.W. Norton, 1999), 15.

112. duCille, *Coupling Convention*, 64, original emphasis.
113. Harper, "The Two Offers," 460, 466.
114. Harper, "The Two Offers," 466.
115. Cornel West, *Race Matters* (Boston: Beacon Press, 2001), 19.
116. Harper, "The Two Offers," 466.

117. I borrow this phrase from Cornel West with David Ritz, *Brother West: Living and Loving Out Loud: A Memoir* (Smiley Books: Carlsbad, 2009).

118. Harper, "The Two Offers," 466.

119. Hildegard Hoeller, "Self-Reliant Women in Frances Harper's Writings," *American Transcendental Quarterly*, 19 (2005): 205–20; quote appears on page 218.

120. Susan Hekman, "The Embodiment of the Subject: Feminism and the Communitarian Critique of Liberalism," *The Journal of Politics*, 54 (1992): 1098–119; quote appears on page 1099.

121. Chris Weedon, *Feminist Practice and Poststructuralist Theory*, Second edition (Malden, Blackwell, 1997), 41.

122. Margaret McLaren, *Feminism, Foucault, and Embodied Subjectivity* (Albany: State University of New York Press, 2002), 76.

123. Harper, "The Two Offers," 461.
124. Peterson argues this point in *Doers of the Word*, 173.
125. Harper, "The Two Offers," 462.

126. Jacqueline Jones Royster, *Traces of a Stream: Literacy and Social Change Among African American Women* (Pittsburgh: University of Pittsburgh Press, 2000), 181.
127. Harper, "The Two Offers," 460.
128. Harper, "The Two Offers," 466.
129. *The Afro-American*, May 9, 1896; Issue 41.
130. Harper, "The Two Offers," 466.
131. Harper, "The Two Offers," 468.
132. Harper, "The Two Offers," 466.

TWO
"Do Unto Others"

De-Racializing the Golden Rule in Julia Collins's
The Curse of Caste; or The Slave Bride

On August 14, 1862, President Abraham Lincoln informed five black leaders gathered at the White House that Congress had appropriated funds "for the purpose of aiding colonization in some country, of the people, or a portion of them, of African descent."[1] The black delegation, composed of "Freemasons, abolitionists, community organizers, AME church leaders, and a "Presbyterian minister,"[2] appeared by invitation to hear the president's prepared remarks. Having surmised the physical difference between blacks and whites to be a "great disadvantage" to both groups, President Lincoln recommended they separate rather than "suffer" in each other's presence.[3] Notably, Lincoln admitted that America afforded whites privileges routinely denied to blacks: "even when you cease to be slaves," he observed to his African American visitors, "you are yet far removed from being placed on an equality with the white race. You are cut off from many of the advantages which the other race enjoy."[4] But rather than eliminate these "advantages," he sought to protect white privilege and purge the U.S. of its black presence. Lincoln proposed Central America as a resettlement destination but unforeseen obstacles derailed colonization efforts and Congress repealed its appropriation in 1864.[5] Lincoln's statement endorsing colonization circulated in the Northern press and angered many black Americans who had long sought full citizenship rights in their native land.[6] As Henry Louis Gates Jr. asserts, Frances E.W. Harper "spoke for many free blacks" when she publicly criticized Lincoln's colonization efforts in the September 27, 1862, issue of the *Christian Recorder*.[7]

Much like Harper, who understood literature as a weapon in black Americans' freedom struggle, Mrs. Julia C. Collins deployed the pen on behalf of her race and took on urgent political issues of her day. Addressing the dignity and value of blackness, Collins's essays and serialized novel could easily be read as complementary to Harper's essay—that is, as an emphatic rejoinder to Lincoln's restrictive racial logic. A teacher living in Williamsport, Pennsylvania, Collins made her debut in the *Christian Recorder* on April 16, 1864, with "Mental Improvement," which was followed by a series of essays on education and racial uplift over the next ten months, and the appearance of her serialized novel, *The Curse of Caste* in February 1865. Literary historians have little access to the details of her life but available records indicate that Collins, a married woman with children, lived in "a predominantly white northern town during the Civil War era."[8] Research has not yet revealed her birth date or the ages of her children, but the September 30, 1865, issue of the *Christian Recorder* prints news of Collins's illness and the hope "that her sickness is not unto death."[9] Shortly thereafter, on December 16, 1865, the magazine announced: "We are sorry to inform our readers that we have received a letter from Mr. S.C. Collins, informing us of the death of his estimable wife, Mrs. Julia C. Collins, authoress of *The Curse of Cast* [sic]; *or, The Slave Bride*."[10] They added, sympathetically, "We know that many of our readers will be greatly disappointed on hearing that they are to be deprived of the pleasure of reading the balance of the beautiful story which she was writing for our paper."[11] Collins had died of tuberculosis on November 25, never submitting the concluding section of her novel or having had an opportunity to publish her story as a book. The novel remains incomplete, but Collins's extant text does much to challenge the "possessive investment in whiteness" evident in Lincoln's segregation scheme, while striving to reimagine restrictive racial identities and hierarchal social relations.[12]

A structural and structuring formation, whiteness has organized bodies, social relations, and national spaces across the course of American history. Charles Mills writes that the "Racial Contract [which underwrites the social contract] establishes a racial polity, a racial state, and a racial juridical system, where the status of whites and nonwhites is clearly demarcated, whether by law or custom."[13] This racial arrangement has historically justified white brutality and innumerable crimes against black bodies. Addressing skeptical readers of the Contract's existence and pinpointing its emergence, Mills explains,

> Far from being lost in the mists of the ages, it is clearly historically locatable in the series of events marking the creation of the modern world by European colonialism and the voyages of "discovery" now increasingly and more appropriately called expeditions of conquest... Thus not only is the Racial Contract "real," but—whereas the social contract is characteristically taken to be establishing the legitimacy of

the nation-state, and codifying morality and law within its boundaries—the Racial Contract is global.[14]

The Racial Contract, then, created a worldwide "racial divide" distinguishing between whites and nonwhites, placing whites atop the racial scale. Since the Contract operates differently across space and time, one necessarily observes "local variations" in its articulation.[15] While Mills, for example, posits "a bipolar racial system in the (Anglo) United States, as against a subtler color hierarchy in (Iberian) Latin America, it remains the case that the white tribe, as the global representation of civilization and modernity, is generally on top of the social pyramid."[16] I quote Mills's argument at length here because Collins's novel actively engages and vigorously questions the inhumane structural practices made possible by the Racial Contract that developed in the United States. Namely, her story does the "cultural work" of interrogating racial assumptions and demarcations, while also questioning what W. E. B. Du Bois has identified as "a sort of public and psychological wage."[17]

The same racism deployed to justify the Racial Contract, rationalize the enslavement of Africans, and concoct Lincoln's separatist racial agenda emerges as a critical issue in *The Curse*. Racism and racially motivated violence result in death and trauma in Collins's allegorical novel, yet her work also articulates the "craving for a better . . . .and nobler existence."[18] In so doing, *The Curse* challenges racist ideology by rendering visible the tragic consequences (psychic and material) of racial values infesting the nation, endorses alternative epistemologies, and advocates the radicalization of "the Golden Rule" into a socially transformative principle.[19] Put another way, she conceptualizes characters who learn to love one another and invites readers to do the same, in the belief that love might affect material change.

"Tarrying with"[20] Collins's representation of love as a variously merciful, antiracist, and anticlassist social force, this chapter draws on affect theory and explores love alongside affective distress in three spaces: slaveholding New Orleans, a Connecticut boarding school, and the Black domestic space. Much like Harper's sentimental story "The Two Offers," *The Curse* appeals to reader sympathy, while fashioning a bond between text and reader to engender progressive racial attitudes and social action. But Collins's uncompleted novel, while progressive, contains contradictions and, further, refuses to present a fully formed vision of a nonracist America. Indeed, even its incompleteness might be said to reflect the nature of incomplete racial understanding. Exploring racial injustice, love, and healing, *The Curse* suggests the impossibility of racial reconciliation pending a conscious national divestment from whiteness—as a dominant structure of social and political authority—and a wholesale reconsideration of "race" in the US imaginary.

The *Curse* was published in thirty-one installments between February 25, 1865, and September 23, 1865, in the *Christian Recorder*,[21] "the most . . . widely distributed African-American newspaper of the nineteenth century."[22] Founded in 1852 as the official organ of the African Methodist Episcopal Church, the weekly paper attracted a largely African American readership.[23]

While the *Recorder* reached even the unexpected reader,[24] Frances Foster Smith and Chanta Haywood assert that "[t]he primary purpose for the 'official organs' of the various denominations was the promotion of each group's particular mission. But the churches' common mission was very much bound up in the political, social, economic and educational progress of its congregants as African-Americans."[25] Devoted to racial uplift activism, which Carla Peterson describes as "improved education, temperance, [and] moral responsibility to self and neighbor,"[26] the *Recorder* published content reinforcing these values; and in the literary texts it published, "[g]enerally the moral and political were merged, suggesting that the resolution of political problems was through the application of morality."[27] Certainly true in the case of *The Curse*, politics has moral implications, and morality informs politics; as such, the story's underlying argument appeals to readers' morals in order to effect sociopolitical change.

Collins's serialized novel, among the first written by a black woman in the U.S., reflects the *Recorder's* commitment to the "diffusion of useful knowledge" among the black community,[28] though it also contains urgent lessons for its considerably smaller white readership. While *The Curse* does not directly engage the Civil War that would soon subside, it positions readers to ponder key philosophical issues bound up with war: race, identity, community, and belonging. As many scholars argue,[29] Collins adapts the genre to address specifically African American concerns; in doing so, she challenges white supremacy, explores the possibility of social change, and endorses an antiracist, anticlassist, love-driven politics. In chapter 1 I quoted bell hooks, who argues that "to truly love we must learn to mix various ingredients—care, affection, recognition, respect, community, and trust, as well as honest and open communication."[30] This chapter draws on her theory and argues that Collins's novel depicts love as an antiracist principle and mode of resistance. As I explore at length in chapter 1, love is an agent of change with the power to engender alternative ways of being-in-the-world. One of the early black writers in a long lineage of literary activists who understood love's transformative power, Collins uses her novel to explore how and why love matters, and reveal how whiteness impedes the ability to love across difference.

Briefly summarized, *The Curse* is set in the antebellum era and tells the story of Lina, a quadroon, who is unaware of her African American ancestry and enslaved condition. While traveling on the Mississippi aboard the steamer Alhambra, she meets and falls in love with Richard Tracy, son of New Orleans plantation owner, Colonel Tracy. Unbeknownst to Lina and Richard, Colonel Tracy subsequently purchases Lina, whom Richard quickly arranges to have his "friend," George Manville, purchase. Shortly thereafter, Richard and Lina depart to Connecticut where they marry and live for half a year, until Richard returns to New Orleans to make peace with his father. Rather than embrace his newly wed son, Colonel Tracy disowns and shoots him. In recovery, Richard writes to Lina but George inexplicably destroys the letter, later informing him that his wife and newborn daughter are dead. Claire, however, survives her mother who died in childbirth, and is subsequently raised by Juno, a black nurse, who once served as Lina's housekeeper. After Claire graduates and, against Juno's wishes, begins work as a governess in the Tracy household, suspicions arise that Claire is Richard's long-lost daughter and Colonel Tracy's black granddaughter. After Claire and the Tracy family undergo much suffering, reflection, and transformation, the story ends optimistically, anticipating Richard's return and family reunification.

WHITENESS AND VIOLENCE

Illuminating how whiteness shapes identity, enabling violence against black (and rebellious white) bodies in the South, Collins critiques the whiteness masquerading as honor in hegemonic versions of masculinity. For most southerners in the Old South, writes Bertram Wyatt-Brown, "honor was inseparable from hierarchy and entitlement, defense of family blood and community needs. All these exigencies required the rejection of the lowly, the alien, and the shamed."[31] Essential elements of southern honor for white southerners of privilege include (but were not limited to) "the inner conviction of self-worth" and "the assessment of the claim by the public."[32] Southern men's self-worth thus hinged on subordinating the Other, defending against threats (perceived or imagined) to one's reputation, and securing the public's favorable opinion. Claiming to live by the "highest ethical standards," white men, except "a few lonely dissenters," embraced an ethical code legitimating racial and class injustice.[33]

Exposing the hypocrisy inherent in this hierarchal social formation, Collins encourages readers to empathize with the "lowly, the alien, and the shamed," whose race or political alliances place them outside the "circle of honor,"[34] and direct their anger toward the oppressor. Slave owner Colonel Tracy, for example, fumes when his son Richard marries Lina, a mixed-race former slave. Fearful that interracial marriage will *dis*honor the family, *dis*-rupt the racial hierarchy, and result in racial leveling, the colonel urges Richard to abandon his "negro" wife.[35] However,

Richard recently returned from the North, where he imbibed several "anti-slavery principles,"[36] counters that he "cannot accede to a proposal that would so deeply involve [his] *honor* and integrity."[37] Desiring and seeing no "*honorable* avenue of escape," Richard insists Lina, a "pure, refined, and good" woman, should "not [be held] responsible for her unfortunate birth."[38] Rejecting his father's hierarchal worldview, Richard redefines the term honorable to encompass antislavery values including "respect[ing] the rights of [his] fellow citizens."[39]

But Richard's racially progressive views mark him as Other within the southern hierarchy, despite his whiteness; his stated views make him alien to the "honorable" approval of slaveholding and denial of black humanity. To rid his home and culture of this alien interloper, Colonel Tracy takes aim at his son and shoots, declaring it matters "not whether [his son] lives or dies."[40] Heeding honor's call, Colonel Tracy endeavors to uphold the racial order and protect his family's bloodline from the perceived pollution of blackness. Such an endeavor suggests that whiteness is an integral part of class privilege.

Colonel Tracy's racialized honor system resonates with what philosopher Robert Birt terms "the bad faith of whiteness."[41] According to Birt, Whiteness is the bad faith identity of the racially dominant. The bad faith of whiteness is the

> self-deception of the privileged, the inauthenticity of dominant people within a racialized social hierarchy. To embrace whiteness is the privilege of exclusive transcendence. But it can live as such only through the denial of the transcendence of an Other, the reduction of that Other to an object . . . At least in America, that Other has been primarily the black. Whiteness could not exist without the Other.[42]

Denying Lina's and Richard's humanity—on the basis of Lina's blackness and her husband's proximity to it—the colonel clearly "flees the truths and perplexities of human existence; in short, he flees himself and alienates himself from others."[43] Reducing complex subjects worthy of dignity to mere objects upon whose subordination his authority depends, the colonel evades the truth of his contingent social position. As Mills notes, "white . . . *misrepresentation, evasion, and self-deception*" are "*prescribed* by the terms of the Racial Contract, which requires a certain schedule of structured blindnesses and opacities in order to establish and maintain the white polity."[44] Arguably, unwilling to "see" humanity in the Other from his structural and ideological position, the colonel brutally punishes Richard for "fail[ing] to live up to the civic and political responsibilities of Whiteness."[45] "Writing in his own blood" on the floor, Richard's vulnerability likely solicits the reader's pity, if not his father's.[46]

In this emotionally charged scene, Collins generates disgust for the enraged, bigoted colonel and evokes sympathy for Richard's socially progressive views. Indeed, in the depiction of Colonel Tracy's racist extremism that drives him to act violently against his own son, Collins astutely uses narrative technique to put the reader in a morally (and in this instance politically) complex and compelling position. According to Wolfgang Iser, writing in a different context, "something happens to us" during the reading process. Namely, "[t]he author's aim . . . is to convey the experience [of the unfamiliar] and, above all, an attitude toward that experience. Consequently, 'identification' is not an end in itself, but a stratagem by means of which the author stimulates attitudes in the reader."[47] Clearly, Collins deploys this strategy perfectly, and in a way that invites, or persuades, readers to identify with the weak and vulnerable—as well as those seeking to aid them—and to be altered by these encounters.

Painting in broad strokes the far-reaching effects of whiteness, the novel details how the colonel's racist violence ripples beyond Richard to harm his entire family: his fragile mother Mrs. Nellie Tracy suffers a breakdown from which she may never recover, his heartsick wife dies during his unexplained absence, and their mixed-raced daughter Claire lives her early years as a lonely orphan. Early in the novel, primary and secondary characters alike testify, chorus-like, to the colonel's inhumanity: his youngest son Lloyd perceives him as "proud"[48]; Juno, the free black nurse who raises Claire, recognizes the colonel's "overweening . . . love of wealth and position,"[49] and his wife Nellie "[stands] somewhat in awe of her lordly husband," whose self-importance engulfs his humanity.[50] Colonel Tracy's inhumanity is seen in other ways as well. His love of power, position, and honor clearly exceeds his love of people, driving him to not only shoot his son but also sever ties with his sister Laura and her "poor" fiancé, Alfred Hays. Their marriage "incur[s] his lasting displeasure" because it violates the hierarchal social order to which he subscribes.[51]

As I argue below, love—manifesting variously as mercy, care, and kindness—emerges as an alternative principle to Colonel Tracy's inhumanity to comfort and facilitate healing for many of these characters. Specifically, when sickly, Lina is granted the gift of mercy; when vulnerable and alone, Claire is offered friendship; and when sad, Mrs. Tracy meets with kindness. In these and other instances, *The Curse* posits expressions of love as a viable response to suffering and social ills. In so doing, the novel calls for a politics of compassion and kindness urgently needed within and beyond its textual borders.

Lacking the quality of imagination Collins encourages readers to develop in her nonfiction texts (also published in the *Christian Recorder*), the colonel perpetuates, beyond racism, a paternalistic tradition in which an organic social hierarchy links but separates masters, their wives, slaves, and children. Historian James Oakes defines paternalism as "the ideological legacy of a feudal political system with no fully developed market economy."[52] This ideology sheds light on the colonel's outlook because, as Virginia Cope argues, paternalism "imagines an organic society of reciprocal relations in which some are born to rule, others to obey. It proved to be an ideal model for defending slavery, for it allowed masters to construe themselves as benevolent caretakers for unavoidably inferior slaves, who as part of an extended household would labor in exchange for protection and guidance."[53] As a wealthy patriarch, Colonel Tracy does not question—but instead revels in—his authority over his wife, children, and slaves—all of whom his power oppresses in explicit and degrading ways. Rather than imagine new forms of engagement premised on principles of justice and equality (as someone not bound up within a paternalistic network of unequal power), he "depends upon the brain-work of others," and so loses his "originality of thought . . . in . . . other men's sentiments," displaying a weakness that Collins laments in her 1864 essay, "A Letter from Oswego: Originality of Ideas."[54]

In effect, the colonel refuses to reflect critically on received systems of power, his materialistic values prevent him from appreciating the intrinsic value of humanity, and his hegemonic version of honor manifests itself as "a heartless, overbearing male passion to rule . . . especially over women and menials."[55] He therefore cuts ties with his sister and shoves her away as she explains that Alfred is "good and noble" despite his poverty.[56] Laura's open-hearted response to her fiancé's poverty makes evident the colonel's narrow-minded bigotry, and encourages readers to reflect critically on Tracy's investment in class privilege. Placing love over greed, she models virtuous behavior worthy of emulation, while the colonel reveals yet another dimension of his cruel inhumanity. This specific passage encourages reader identification with Laura (who, as a woman, is subject to her brother's patriarchal power) and provides an impetus for reading aright the colonel's prejudices.

Colonel Tracy's "closed" disposition is perhaps best symbolized by Collins's depiction of the locked library at the family plantation. Normally a site for learning and growth, the inaccessible library can only be opened by the colonel (who had not crossed the "blood-stained threshold" for "years") and his wife, as he "has forbidden any one to visit the library."[57] Signifying the colonel's power over the plantation's inhabitants and his desire to forbid their access to knowledge, the locked library highlights his close-minded ignorance and unwillingness to reimagine inequitable social relations.

In her multifaceted critique of southern white male power, Collins not only exposes the plantation patriarch as dishonorable and narrow-minded but she also depicts him as cowardly—the very opposite of the celebrated mythical honorable southerner.[58] Colonel Tracy illuminates this contradiction when grief ultimately drives him secretly to visit the library to gaze upon his alienated son's portrait; notably, he "does not wish to be observed" by his family in the act, nor does he wish to invite "unpleasant comments" from his slaves. He thus "steal[s] through his own house like a thief, at midnight," hoping to reach his destination, unseen.[59] Here again, Collins highlights the colonel's excessive concern with others' opinion. Readers will recall he "was horrified" when his son voiced "antislavery principles" in the presence of his "acquaintances" and he now wishes to avoid even innocuous inquiries from his family and slaves.[60] Underscoring how "honor . . . made the opinion of others inseparable from inner worth,"[61] Collins contrasts the timid colonel unfavorably with Richard, a markedly brave southerner possessing "a mind and soul susceptible of improvement and cultivation."[62]

While Colonel Tracy's life shrinks into cowardice, fear, and loneliness, Richard's independence and imaginativeness stand in sharp relief to his father's mindless dependence on tradition. Ultimately, Richard's lively spirit emboldens him to reject his father's racism and classism and denounce the "accursed" institution of slavery.[63] While Richard's antiracist voice recedes in the book's later chapters, his liberalism offers hope for change and represents a radical thread knitting together Collins's chapters.

WHITENESS AND REMORSE

The Curse underlines the ideology of whiteness and its tragic effects on society's Others but goes further, examining the ways racism can boomerang, backfiring on the representative slaveholder. As historian James Oliver Horton notes, Thomas Jefferson "argued that, from his point of view, one of the worst things about slavery was its corruption of whites."[64] Harriet Jacobs's *Incidents in the Life of a Slave Girl* sheds further light on this dynamic from the female slave's perspective:

> The slaveholder's sons are, of course, vitiated, even while boys, by the unclean influences every where around them. Nor do the master's daughters always escape. Severe retributions sometimes come upon him for the wrongs he does to the daughters of the slaves. The white daughters early hear their parents quarrelling about some female slave. Their curiosity is excited, and they soon learn the cause. They are attended by the young slave girls whom their father has corrupted; and they hear such talk as should never meet youthful ears, or any other ears. They know that the women slaves are subject to their father's authority in all things; and in some cases they exercise the same authority over the men slaves.[65]

Jacobs and Collins employ different genres, the slave narrative and fiction, yet both writers detail the damage racism wreaks on slaveholders and their families. As Jacobs notes above, white sons emulate their lascivious slaveholding fathers, who rape their slaves, betray their wives, and inadvertently instill corrupt principles in their young daughters. In this sense, racism turns on itself, debasing those who deploy it to oppress others. In her novel, Collins boldly takes on the self-contradictory nature of racism in the chapter titled "Remorse." By the novel's mid-point, the colonel has become a shadow of his former self. "[T]hinner and paler,"[66] his "haggard face bespoke great mental suffering,"[67] while his "proud form is slightly bowed."[68] The narrator clearly states the colonel has aged but implies his racially motivated violence against his son has hastened the process. For example, the narrative invites readers to contrast the narrow-minded colonel's condition with that of Dr. Singleman, the racially progressive white character who tends Richard's gun-inflicted wound. Strikingly, the physician has changed but "slightly" over the years and "presents a pleasing picture of healthy old age,"[69] whereas the colonel, whose "pale brow" is "bathed" in perspiration,[70] "liv[es] under a shadow."[71] As such, Collins subtly links the colonel's anxiety, sadness, and premature aging to his bigotry and guilt-laden conscience.

In "Memory and Imagination," an essay published in the *Recorder* in 1865, Collins articulates a principle shedding light on the colonel's condition: "[i]f we steadfastly practise [sic] the 'Golden Rule,' let it guide and govern our lives; we shall have few dark pictures to mourn over."[72] Since Colonel Tracy disregarded the "rule" and instead practiced a racialized honor ethic, he necessarily dwells on the "dark pictures" Collins warns of. Namely, he fixates on his absent son and sees Claire's face "follow[ing] [him] like an avenging spirit."[73] For years, he had managed to "banish all thought" of shooting his son but "[r]emorseless memory dragged to light those scenes he had been for years striving to forget."[74] Now a "guilty, wretched man," he "commun[es] with his own sad thoughts" for "hours" at a time.[75] Arguably, intense, private suffering marks a breakthrough for the colonel as "[h]onor, not conscience, and [public] shame, not guilt, were the psychological and social underpinnings of Southern culture."[76] Notably breaking from this tradition, the colonel confronts his conscience, acknowledges his crime, and begins grappling privately with his guilt. In agony, he cries: "Oh, Richard, my son! my punishment is indeed greater than I can bear! . . . My *curse* has recoiled upon my own head."[77] Experiencing what modern readers might call depression, the colonel passes hours "absorbed in grief."[78] But it might be more appropriate to call it productive grief, for it pushes him to face long denied truths: he comes to recognize that he wronged Richard, to contemplate his mysterious relation to Claire, and to realize that his "vast possessions" have "failed to bring him happiness."[79] Still and significantly, the Colonel fails to disavow altogether racism and materialism in this scene of suffering; nor does he display the expected empathy for others, but he does look upon the "ruin" that had "nestled like a canker worm at his heart."[80] In subsequent chapters addressed below, Colonel Tracy strives to uproot this "worm" of bigotry and replace it with loving-kindness for the Other. Having experienced the consequences of his own racially motivated violence, he works to repair the damage inflicted by building bridges between himself and those he once rejected. Specifically, his other-directed care for Claire resembles bell hooks's definition of love as "the will to extend one's self for the purpose of nurturing one's own or another's spiritual growth."[81]

AFFECTIVE DISTRESS AND REDEMPTIVE LOVE

In chapter 1, I quoted psychologist Silvan Tomkins, who writes the "major sources of distress throughout life arise from the body, its pains and illnesses, from work and its problems, and from the vicissitudes of interpersonal relationships. The environment is constantly also creating new disturbances and challenges which create distress."[82] Tomkins further observes that "crying expresses suffering 'both bodily pain and mental distress'" and that one of the "biological functions of crying" is "to motivate . . . others to do something to reduce the crying response."[83] Emphasizing the sociality of affect, Tomkins asserts one who cares for another readily sees and strives to alleviate the loved one's distress. In the absence of positive affect, however, a relation of identification must be cultivated to motivate action on behalf of the suffering.[84] Such is Collins's charge. In *The Curse*, Collins works to "stimulate attitudes" resulting in identification with and compassion for figures who suffer in the novel.[85]

Many characters in *The Curse* undergo distress arising from the broken body, strained relations, and garden-variety hardships—challenges the novel suggests love can lessen, if not rectify. In the boarding school, the black domestic space, and on the Tracy family plantation, distress throws characters' lives into crisis. In response, love often emerges variously as care, kindness, sympathy, and compassion, soothing emotional and physical wounds. In chapter 1, Collins outlines (but does not circumscribe) parameters for her love-driven politics. Specifically, after graduating from seminary, Claire Neville informs her friend Ella Summers that she is a mere "child of poverty and misfortune."[86] Distressed at the prospect of "leaving old friends and associations, to go forth into a cold and uncharitable world," Claire tearfully shares her impoverished condition with Ella, a "child of wealth and position."[87] As Veta Tucker writes, "a number of elements in this opening scene correspond to what Nina Baym theorized as the "overplot of nineteenth-century woman's fiction."[88] Namely, Claire, a poor orphan, must venture into the world alone as she "is losing the financial support of a benefactor and the emotional support of a surrogate family."[89] To Claire's astonishment, however, Ella insists that she "love[s] [her] now better than ever" and again encourages Claire to "make the [previously] proposed visit" to her house for the summer.[90] Ella's sympathy increases upon learning of Claire's poverty and thus models a mode of being for readers encountering similarly distressed individuals. Much like the colonel's open-minded sister Laura, Ella prioritizes character over economic status, "model[ing] how sympathy for others could mediate the differences between . . . rich and poor." [91] Ella is privileged and Claire is working class, but kindness compels her to comfort rather than reject her friend; in doing so, Claire is consoled and Ella models a potentially subversive practice inherently critiquing the hierarchal socioeconomic order.

In her groundbreaking *Sensational Designs*, Jane Tompkins asserts that literary texts "attempt to redefine the social order."[92] The sentimental texts she examines "have designs upon their audiences, in the sense of wanting to make people think and act in a particular way."[93] In this spirit, Collins links modes of feeling, thinking, and acting, endeavoring to inspire more compassionate relations across gender, race, and class lines. The "world of feeling" percolating in sentimental literature has a long and complex history explored by a significant body of scholarship. In eighteenth-century Britain, the term "sentimentalism" was coined,[94] but it would quickly traverse the Atlantic and find resonance on American soil.

Taking William H. Brown's *The Power of Sympathy* (1789) as an example, Elizabeth Barnes claims that "the early American novel cannot be understood if separated from the sentimental ideology out of which it arises or from eighteenth-century theories of interpersonal dynamics of which sentimentalism forms a part."[95] Barnes defines sentimental ideology as "the cultural expression of the desire for union,"[96] a longing emerging dramatically in Collins's novel as Claire's yearning for family reunion and knowledge of her ancestral origins. Furthermore, Barnes invokes Paine's *Common Sense* (1776) and Adam Smith's "Theory of Moral Sentiments" (1759), both of which privilege sentiment for specific ends; Paine, for example, "employs the rhetoric of filial loyalty in order to explain and justify the colonists' desire to protect (or expand) their economic interests,"[97] while Smith theorizes the "sympathetic identification" allowing a person to connect imaginatively with one who suffers.[98] Convincingly, Barnes links sentimental literature and eighteenth-century theories of interpersonal relations with sentimental ideology.

Using the language of sympathy, these works cultivate an other-oriented ethos consistent with sentimentalism, which "psychologically connect[s] an individual to things and people outside him or her."[99] Deploying this literary convention, Collins privileges unity as a key theme in her novel, and as a central principle underlying her appeal to potentially sympathetic readers. Put another way, Collins depicts sympathetic relations between characters and strives to cultivate an emotional bond with readers.[100] Her characters evoke from each other and readers a range of feelings from sympathy and empathy to compassion.

The argument I am making here may be made clearer by a brief historical consideration of several key conceptual categories that are central to my thinking. The *Oxford English Dictionary* defines sympathy as "the quality or state of being affected by the condition of another with a feeling similar or corresponding to that of the other . . . . fellow-feeling." Sympathy as employed here thus means to *feel for* or suffer with another; I use Martha C. Nussbaum's definition of empathy as "the imaginative reconstruction of another person's experience, without any particular evaluation of that experience,"[101] which makes clear that we cannot fully feel another's feelings. Lindsay B. Cummings elaborates that "[e]mpathy need not consist, as some have described it, of putting yourself in someone else's shoes (thereby assuming a correspondence between your reaction and theirs), but might instead involve using all that you understand about the other to imagine *her* feelings and reactions in that particular situation."[102] Imagination plays a key role in Nussbaum's definition of compassion, which she uses interchangeably with the word "pity."[103] Drawing on the classic understanding of emotion, Nussbaum observes, "as Aristotle argued long ago, human compassion standardly requires three thoughts: that a serious bad thing has happened to someone else; that this bad event was not (or not entirely) the person's own fault; and that we ourselves are vulnerable in similar ways. Thus compassion forms a psychological link between our own self-interest and the reality of another person's good or ill."[104] She argues further that a "crucial part of the ethical value of pity is its ability to cross boundaries of class, nationality, race, and gender, as the pitier assumes these different positions in imagination, and comes to see the obstacles to flourishing faced by human beings in these many concrete situations."[105]

Collins exhibits this sort of understanding about affect in *The Curse*, presenting a range of emotions to call forth compassionate action on behalf of a select group of whites and (as I discuss, below) African Americans. Importantly, Nussbaum argues, compassion "provides an essential bridge from self-interest to just conduct."[106] Collins constructs such a bridge in her textual world, by encouraging readers to feel and act differently. Some scholars, however, view sentimentality and sympathy differently. A significant body of scholarship vigorously critiques sentimentality and its attendant "fellow feelings," raising valid concerns about their implementation. Laura Wexler details the "violence" sentimentalism wreaks as it "encourages a large-scale imaginative depersonalization of those outside its complex significations"[107] and enabled the ruthless cultural indoctrination of black and Native Americans in the nineteenth century,[108] while Saidiya Hartman asserts that nineteenth-century representations of suffering slaves too easily invited narcissistic identification between readers and textual Others, rather than historically situated humane recognition.[109] These arguments sound clear warnings against unethical (and perhaps other unintended uses) of sentimentality. While the limitations of sentimentalism emerge periodically in Collins's narrative, *The Curse* nonetheless makes a compelling case for love's power and labors to build what Nussbaum calls the "bridge from self-interest to just conduct."

Benevolence, as kindness, generally shapes Claire's boarding school experience where she has been "happy in the love of her schoolmates and kind preceptress, Miss Ellwood."[110] Notably, her classmates' and mentor's kindness have affective, joy-producing power, muting the potential effects of "the bitter isolation of her life."[111] In "Happy Objects," Sara Ahmed "consider[s] happiness as a happening, as involving affect (to be affected by something), intentionality (to be happy is to be happy about something), and evaluation or judgment (to be happy about something makes something good)."[112] Claire, who judged these figures of compassion as "good," experiences *"increase[d] pleasure, or diminish[ed] pain"* in their presence.[113] Anticipating that Claire may encounter hardships in her future position as governess, her friend urges, "do not forget your Ella," and the girls part after "a loving embrace."[114] This encouragement to *remember* links up with Collins's argument in "Memory and Imagination": "By the aid of memory we are enabled to review the past, from our infancy. We may dwell long and lovingly over the sweet scenes of our childhood, as fond recollection presents them to view."[115] Indeed, in a subsequent scene of despair discussed below, Claire reconnects imaginatively with Ella, Juno, and Miss Ellwood to soothe her suffering spirit. They become "happy objects" Claire can recall in the midst of sadness. Punctuated by acts of loving kindness, chapter 1 sets the stage for compassionate acts that follow, positioning readers to respond dually: to pity the distressed and emulate characters espousing a compassionate countercultural ethos.

The Curse not only features interracial intimacy (between Lina and Richard) and cross-class communion (between Claire and Ella) but also depicts loving intra-racial support as a critical social practice between black women in despair (including those who are legally "black" and phenotypically white). Specifically, the narrative positions Juno Hayes (an African American whose first name derives from Roman mythology and means goddess of women and motherhood) as a primary caregiver to Lina (a quadroon) and her daughter Claire (an octoroon). She "had taken care of [Claire] as long as she could remember," for example, raising her until she turned twelve and was sent to the "L—Seminary."[116] She tends to Claire, looking after her during her formative years; and after Claire graduates and insists on working as a governess in the Tracy home, Juno assures her she will "never cease to pray for [her]."[117] Yet long before raising Claire, Juno works as housekeeper in Lina's home, where she did more than keep house. Watching over Lina who waits, in a distressed state, for Richard (who is visiting his father in New Orleans) to write, Juno "shed[s] tears of sympathy with that fragile creature that leaned heavily on her arm."[118] Her ardent love for Lina compels her to honor her employer's deathbed request to "[b]e faithful to my child, Juno;

never forsake her."[119] Trusting Juno to be a constant, loyal figure in her daughter's life, Lina seals a permanent bond between Juno and her child. In a selfless act of mercy and compassion, Juno chooses to raise Claire almost like a daughter.

Sustaining nourishing relations with other women of African descent, Juno exemplifies the critical role black women can play for each other. As Eric Gardner writes, Juno "tr[ies] to protect Lina and then Claire—and to build a life for herself."[120] Moreover, argues Gardner, "the love between Juno and Claire is deep and lasting: when Claire visits before going South, 'Juno was delighted to see her dear child,' . . . and 'the parting, between the faithful old nurse and the child she had watched over so long, was touching in the extreme.'"[121] This scene proves especially moving within the world of sentiment. As Joanne Dobson writes, "Sentimentalism envisions the self-in-relation; family (not necessarily in the conventional biological sense), intimacy, community, and social responsibility are its primary relational modes."[122] Though Juno is not her biological mother, Claire has warm feelings for her "old beloved nurse,"[123] who wholly reciprocates her love and through whom she clarifies her own emotions. For instance, Juno sympathizes with Claire and *feels for* her, stating, "I hope you may be happy"[124]; significantly, "Claire felt Juno's words to be an echo of her own feelings."[125] Almost as if connected at the heart, these women resonate on an emotional plane.

Privileging loving bonds between black women who value *each other*, the novel simultaneously depicts *Blackness* as lovable. In the same vein, Juno's relationship with her African American husband, Martin Ray, is presented as a viable, loving partnership. Martin is a *"worthy"* and virtuous man with "unlimited confidence in his wife's opinion."[126] He good-naturedly and repeatedly helps interpret her dreams and the two "lived quietly and happily together."[127] Modeling healthy partnership and non-hierarchal ways of being-in-the-world, they listen to and trust each other. In *Friendship: A History*, Barbara Caine describes Aristotle's concept of "virtue-friendship," which resonates with Juno's and Martin's union. Virtue-friendship "arises when we love another as someone who is good or virtuous."[128] Aristotle identifies this relation as the "best form of friendship,"[129] and "complete" as "it is the friendship of good people similar in virtue, for they wish goods in the same way to each other, insofar as they are good."[130] Unambiguously represented as "good," decent people invested in each other's (as well as others') well-being, Juno and Martin model respectful devotion, and attentive friendship, underscoring the humanity and value of blackness.

Intra-racial compassion emerges periodically in the novel and has real-world implications for nineteenth-century black readers. In 1865, black families separated and displaced by slavery relied heavily on local support systems and institutions even as they attempted to reunite with loved ones. According to Heather Williams, "[f]ollowing the war, African

Americans used the new black and Republican newspapers to help carry out their search."[131] Some blacks could pen their own ads while "others would have received help from a literate person in their community,[132] and some turned to their hometown ministers for support.[133] In the *Christian Recorder*, as Jean Lee Cole notes, "escaped slaves placed ads—with the customary headline, "Information Wanted"—describing long-lost relatives in the hopes of finding them."[134] Moreover, Cole writes, there was a "general reluctance on the part of the northern black elite to embrace the newly freed population—due, in part, to a willfully maintained ignorance of them. This reluctance was noticeable to both whites and blacks."[135] As such, black readers, North and South, elite and poor, might have recognized and found relevant to their own lives the intra-communal love connecting Juno, Lina, and Martin Ray. While Collins depicts tender relations between these black and mixed raced-characters, she fails to imagine intimate ties among upwardly mobile blacks and the broader community of slaves laboring on the Tracy plantation, perhaps suggesting the limitations of her cultural imagination. Thus intra-racial compassion between blacks plays a key role but in limited social contexts, as I explore below.

Within a racialized textual world, Juno's commitment to loving (three) other black characters combines with self-regard, making what can be interpreted as an affirmative statement on black identity. The narrator describes Juno as "a competent colored woman,"[136] and as Gardner rightly argues, readers' racial identification with Juno might . . . have been a minefield. Juno is, after all, *not* the novel's heroine and not the main character."[137] Moreover, "the position Juno potentially occupies vis-a-vis the 'white' and 'clear' Claire carries resonances of 'Mammy' stereotypes, the Aunt Chloe of *Uncle Tom's Cabin*, and/or the generations of enslaved Black women forced to care for white children even as their own children were separated from them or simply stolen from them."[138]

At the same time, Juno extends love not only to Lina and Claire (the phenotypically white characters) but also to her black husband and *herself*. In doing so, she potentially distinguishes herself from the traditional mammy figure, the black woman considered "[l]oyal, docile, but fiercely protective of her white folks, [who] exalted in her servitude."[139] Cognizant of her own value, for example, she balks at the prospect of black inferiority and exclaims she "doesn't see why black blood ain't just as good as white any day!"[140] In call-and-response fashion, and affirming Juno's wisdom, the narrator answers, "Unsophisticated Juno, others have asked the same question."[141]

Unlike Colonel Tracy, Juno resists hierarchal identity frameworks, reflects critically on received racial truths, and endorses a counterhegemonic viewpoint positing blacks and whites as equals. Interestingly, Juno withholds from Claire knowledge of her blackness, as she "always thought it best that Claire should never know she was tainted with black blood."[142] But as Jennifer Rae Greeson argues, "[w]ith Juno, Collins hypothesizes the necessary conditions for a happy resolution of the present action in the novel: not hiding the fact that Claire is 'tainted with black blood'—as did those who attempted to protect Lina—but rather fighting the erroneous assumption" that white blood is superior to black "will save Claire from living out a repetition of her mother's fate."[143] Thus, Juno vehemently refuses to internalize white-supremacist values and pass them on to Claire. Recognizing blackness as a valuable subject position, Juno disrupts dominant discourses that demean and denigrate her race. Reinforcing the *Christian Recorder*'s goal of "articulating a sense of racial consciousness and solidarity unbound by differences of denomination, region, and gender,"[144] Juno establishes solidarity with other black women and ascribes positive value to blackness. In these ways, Juno both surpasses and challenges the stereotypical notion of the mammy figure found in so much literature of the period. Her love, sympathy, and benevolence are embedded in, and arise from, a strong sense of dignity and self-worth.

Despite Juno's enduring love and faithful prayers for her young charge, Claire's ignorance of her parents' identity produces profound despair and suffering, rendering her worthy of both characters' and readers' sympathy. Bearing in mind Claire's distress stems from Colonel Tracy's refusal to accept a mixed-raced daughter-in-law in the first place, readers recall the harmful effects of whiteness on the Tracy family (including Claire, herself). Evoking sympathy, the narrator describes the "delirious" young woman as longing desperately for details of her parentage: "Sometimes she raved . . . of Juno, and her northern home. Sometimes she called plaintively for Miss Elwood; then she would hold long talks with her dear friend, Ella Summers. Again she would ask, in ringing tones: 'Who am I? Oh, some one tell me! This suspense will kill me.'"[145] In her distressed state, Claire imaginatively "turns toward" a cross-racial, cross-class community of caregivers and friends whose proven kindness gave her past solace.[146] As Ahmed notes in her study on affect, one "can just recall pleasure to experience pleasure, even if these pleasures do not involve exactly the same sensation"[147] While Claire continues "suffering" and displays no immediate external signs of relief from her sorrow,[148] I would suggest thoughts of Juno and her preceptress, in addition to "talks" with Ella provide some measure of comfort. Highlighting Claire's mental state and physical body, this text informs readers, "It seemed almost in vain that the queenly little head was shorn of its wealth of purple black hair," and directs their gaze to that "well-shaped head, shorn of its crowning glory."[149] A sentimental project "about imagining the nation's bodies,"[150] *The Curse* uses Claire's grief and bout with "brain fever" to evoke reader sympathy for her exposed body and pitiful condition—and to stir up anger for the colonel whose racism produced her crisis.[151]

Claire's suffering drives her into the Tracy family's loving arms—a unity many scholars argue symbolizes post-civil war racial reconciliation. During her convalescence, "[e]very one, from the stern old Colonel down to the youngest urchin about the establishment, seemed desirous of doing something to show their love for the young creature."[152] I shall discuss the implications of the Colonel's surprising solicitousness below, but for now will note simply that he "was always thinking of something that would add to her comfort,"[153] along with the entire Tracy family: Nellie, who "refused to be comforted" collaborates with the slave Jim to take the ailing Claire a tray of food[154]; Mrs. Tracy "spent the most of her time by the couch upon which the invalid reclined," and even the envious Isabelle, "who seldom visited the sick-room, now asked, in a cold, formal manner, each morning, after Claire's health."[155] The family's steady, sustained attention resonates with hooks's understanding of love: extending "one's self for the purpose of nurturing one's own or another's spiritual growth."[156] Since "[p]oor Claire had a warm place in many hearts,"[157] the Tracys express their love by rallying to alleviate her suffering and anticipate her needs. This scene of unity could well reflect the hope of African Americans' eventual acknowledgement and recognition as part of the national "family."

Gardner and Tomeiko Ashford Carter, respectively, analyze effectively what motivates the family's loving behavior.[158] Gardner persuasively argues "[t]he learning Nellie shows (and gains) here—rooted in domesticity and love, embodied in the sharing of food, and aided by a Black presence—is deeply consonant with what Juno seems to have taught Claire in her youth"[159]; and Carter correctly suggests "the successful outcome of Claire's reliance on prayer signifies that she possesses a specific spiritual agency wielded particularly as she encounters various characters and especially as she interacts with various members of the Tracy household.[160] I underscore and elaborate on Mrs. Tracy and Colonel Tracy's response to Claire's loving presence. As "governess and companion to an invalid,"[161] Claire tends to both Mrs. Tracy and her daughters. In return, Mrs. Tracy learns to "love" Claire "for [her]self alone," having "learned to know her gentle heart."[162] Claire's kindness has profoundly impacted Mrs. Tracy, who places complete confidence in Claire's "sensitive heart" and trusts the young woman will "sympathize with [her]" in her suffering.[163] Mrs. Tracy and her children love Claire because she has befriended, soothed, and comforted them. Their displays of love during Claire's time of need remind readers of their own ability to bestow kindness upon society's most vulnerable members. But what are readers to make of Colonel Tracy's unexpected compassion for the orphaned biracial young woman?

While *The Curse* acknowledges the sin of whiteness as a cultural formation, it also explores the possibility of unlearning racism and developing loving acceptance for the Other. Namely, Colonel Tracy early insists on the "absurdity of entertaining such notions as social equality between races so widely divergent, in every respect, as the white and black,"[164] and shoots Richard for refusing to abandon his mixed-race wife. Racist ideology robs the Colonel of his humanity and so he dehumanizes those who reject his regressive racial views. The widespread and dramatic consequences of his racism help reinforce Collins's antiracist goals, for the Colonel's reckless actions alter for the worse the course of several characters' lives. Significantly, Collins introduces marked psychological suffering as a crucial stage in the racial reconciliation process. It is the Colonel's recognition of wrongdoing and subsequent suffering that help produce his solicitous "remorseful tenderness" toward Claire.[165]

On the nature of suffering, Pope John Paul II writes that "[f]ollowing the parable of the Gospel, we could say that suffering, which is present under so many different forms in our human world, is also present in order *to unleash love in the human person*, that unselfish gift of one's 'I' on behalf of other people, especially those who suffer."[166] As mentioned above, the Colonel spends time "communing with his own sad thoughts" because he *must*—he cannot escape into the "[o]blivion [which] would be a heaven."[167] His period of inescapable sadness prepares him to choose love rather than racism and to extend his "I" for the good of others. After a prolonged and deep sadness, the Colonel is able to greet Claire (who is also suffering) with a "strange blending of tenderness and formality,"[168] which subsequently transmogrifies into a desire to show his "love."[169] Independently confirming his character development, "[a]ll, except Richard [who hasn't seen his father in years] thought that the Colonel's pride was pretty well subdued."[170] No longer privileging the "I," in which he once took such pride, the Colonel strives to address Claire's needs. To put a finer point on it, after realizing "beyond the least semblance of a doubt" that Claire is his granddaughter,[171] he is "always thinking of something that would add to her comfort."[172] While the colonel's individual transformation toward his (legally) black grandchild reflects the "Golden Rule's" injunction to "do unto others as you would have them do unto you" (Matthew 7:12), he nevertheless remains part of the problem as a plantation patriarch entrenched in the system of slavery.

Contrasting with the Colonel who instigates much suffering, the progressive Dr. Singleton strives to alleviate it and further demonstrates how sentimental feelings can enable compassionate action. The doctor, for example, "gazes with compassion" upon Richard shortly after the Colonel shoots him. Emphasizing the power of sentiment, "[t]he pleading glance of [Richard's] bright, dark eyes, went straight to the doctor's heart."[173] Richard's suffering affects his emotions and shortly thereafter, Dr. Singleton "determined to befriend the young man . . . who, he believed, was worthy of his deepest sympathy."[174] Having judged Richard—who resembles physically his own son who died "among strangers"—to be a "noble youth,"[175] he feels deeply for the suffering young man. Tellingly, the doctor first identifies with Richard and *then* develops feeling for him. Uniting emotions with timely action, Dr. Singleton promptly restores Richard to health. This encounter illustrates compassion under ideal conditions but such interactions can also go awry. As Nussbaum observes,

> Sometimes, too, compassion goes wrong by getting the seriousness of the bad event wrong: Sometimes, for example, we just don't take very seriously the hunger and illness of people who are distant from us. These errors are likely to be built into the nature of compassion as it develops in childhood and then adulthood: We form intense attachments to the local first, and only gradually learn to have compassion for people who are outside our own immediate circle.[176]

Since Richard reminds Dr. Singleton of his own son, we might characterize his attachment to Richard as "local," but Collins's ultimate goal includes getting readers to identify with people rather unlike themselves—from different racial and class backgrounds. In this case, Dr. Singleton allows Collins to demonstrate the power of sympathetic identification where positive affect already exists. This scene of sympathy, that is, affects the doctor's heart and reaches for the reader's: "Thus, Richard unconsciously won for himself a warm friend—one who was destined greatly to influence his after life [*sic*]; and thus it is, in life, we sometimes unconsciously win friendship."[177] Constructing a textual community with the pronoun "we," the narrative voice resonates with hope that readers may someday also benefit from (or be generous enough to extend) such kindness.

Collins's invocation of the "Golden Rule" resonates with broader Christian implications informing *The Curse*. As Joycelyn Moody argues, "the term sentimental applies to literature that paradoxically both assumes and seeks to bring about an emotional and moral alliance between reader and text . . . an intimacy that is rooted in common cultural assumptions about virtue and piety."[178] Religion was critical to the early sentimental project as early white women writers "saw the patriarchal Christianity of eighteenth-century America as an integral component of sentimentalism" and subsequently "engag[e] sentimentalism to indict patriarchy for its impediments to women's equal rights."[179] While many white women challenged patriarchal relations in their texts, Christianity has been put to many uses since eighteenth-century developments. In *The Caste*, Collins engages in a sentimental project that disrupts Southern white male power and also attempts to evoke sympathy and compassion for the suffering. As Moody writes in a different context, "[t]his effect clearly depends on authors and readers sharing both a common Christian moral code."[180] Assuming spiritual compatibility with her readers, Collins embeds religious discourse and subjectivity throughout her text to reinforce this spiritual bond. From the narrator's pious observations to Claire's prayerfulness, and Juno's gratitude for God's earthly intervention, Collins constructs a Christian worldview privileging Christian values including love, faith, and kindness in a sentimental framework. In depicting figures distressed or damaged by racialism, she endeavors to "convert" readers to her Christian ideals and call forth affective responses.

The novel's progressive elements, however, exist in tension with its conservative representation of the Tracy family's slaves.[181] In this sense, we might read *The Curse* as a "literary weapon" that Collins uses *selectively* to wage war against racial stereotypes. Specifically, she depicts mixed-race and upwardly mobile African Americans as full of the "spirit of improvement, and self-elevation" of which she writes approvingly in "Intelligent Women," while representing slaves (in general) as flat, buffoonish characters content in their servitude.[182] Namely, Collins depicts both Juno and her husband as hardworking, respectable, and upwardly mobile. Presenting a cozy image of black domesticity for the inhabitants of the "neat little cottage,"[183] the kitchen, replete with "snowy" chairs, "rows of shining tins, and polished cooking stove," all reflect Juno's commitment to maintaining a clean and orderly home. "Baskets filled with newly washed muslins" await Juno's "deft hands," testifying to her industrious spirit and general competence, and she is appropriately paired with Martin Ray, an "industrious man."[184] Hardworking, disciplined, and responsible, Juno and Martin exemplify the Puritan work ethic and represent upwardly mobile blacks' ability to prosper in national community. Similarly, mixed-raced Lina, "educated at a Catholic school in Canada,"[185] is intelligent, modest, "good and pure."[186] She possesses a "voice of sweet and thrilling power" and decorates her home with impeccable taste.[187] Her daughter Claire, whose "musical powers were highly cultivated," has "great talent for music, both vocal and instrumental."[188] That she was well-educated at the "L—Seminary" and proves smart enough to teach white children on the Tracy's plantation,[189] represents former slaves (Lina) and their offspring (Claire) as ideal members of the national community.

Unfortunately, Collins's depictions of the Tracy's slaves starkly contrast with these positive renderings of blackness and biraciality. Variously described demeaningly as a "group of weeping negroes," comically as "a troop of frightened negroes, whose dusky faces thronged every available door and window,"[190] and as an undifferentiated body that "looked gloomy with their sad, dusky faces,"[191] the slave population appears less than fully human. Tucker agrees, arguing it represents them in the same ways "slaves are represented in conventional southern plantation novels."[192] Such negative depictions suggest Collins's primary rhetorical concern is with the fate of black and mixed-raced persons preparing for fully enfranchised citizenship in the postwar nation. Like other advocates of black uplift, she arguably hinged vindication of the race on the example provided by its more privileged members, a connection that, as Kevin Gaines has argued, entailed disidentification with the black poor in the postbellum era.[193] Collins's rhetorical move perhaps evinces what bell hooks terms a "major blind spo[t]"[194]—a site of oppression activists overlook while addressing causes they prioritize. While I do not equate Collins's literary maneuvers with "feminist white women who work daily to eradicate sexism" while failing to engage racism,[195] I would suggest that Collins apparently privileges the needs of upwardly mobile blacks (like herself) at the expense of enslaved characters, thus implying their unworthiness of serious literary engagement. Seemingly, Collins cannot fully escape the cultural and ideological constraints of the period in which she was writing, yet her impulse is toward progressive change.

An alternative interpretation might read Collins's depiction as a critique of systemic inequality and a refusal to equate the advancement of a few with the improvement of the masses. Consider how Lina's and Claire's status improves dramatically during the course of the narrative: Lina transitions from slave to beloved wife, and Claire from a lonely orphan to a potential Count's wife; while Juno and her husband's notable domestic bliss promises more of the same. But these individual advancements are insufficient to empower the masses and unable to mitigate systemic inequality. While the lot of relatively privileged individuals has improved, Collins seems to suggest, the unequal system remains intact and must be dismantled for justice to prevail.

Despite seeming contradictions, Collins's novel challenges the U.S. racial order in meaningful and at times radical ways, engaging philosophical concerns that occupy Harper in "The Two Offers." The founders of the nation did not include blacks, women, and the poor in their vision of national solidarity but Collins envisions the extension of sympathy and affection to human subjects across the lines of race, gender, and caste; Lina, Claire, Laura, and her impoverished husband Alfred are represented as fully human beings worthy of kindness, mercy, and compassion. Moreover, the representative slaveholder learns to love and embrace his mixed-raced grandchild. Radicalizing the "Golden Rule," the novel promotes an antiracist, love-driven politics striking a hopeful note for social change. Importantly, Claire's last words in the final chapter reinforce the possibility of better times to come: "And I am happy," she murmurs, joyously anticipating her long-lost father's arrival.[196] Affected "in a good way," Claire "turns toward" the vision of the "happy family" where "difference is reconciled."[197] Awash in good feelings, Claire indeed "embodies hope for national regeneration," as Gabrielle Foreman aptly claims.[198]

Read as a symbolic representation of social life at a particular historical moment, the novel recommends the nation confront the consequences of whiteness as Colonel Tracy does, so as to interrupt the racial violence (psychic and material) and initiate a period of national healing. Fully aware that gender and whiteness operated as the condition of American citizenship, Collins urges readers black and white to reject patriarchal systems of power, rethink racial logic, and fulfill the tenets of the Golden Rule. But at the uncompleted novel's end, Colonel Tracy remains a plantation owner deriving his wealth from slave labor. For all his individual kindness to Claire, he remains a symbol of corrupt and pervasive power. Collins thus makes clear that a truly "new" nation requires the reconstruction of society and reimagining of social identities—not as a barrier to inclusion, but as a bridge to self-discovery and meaningful reconciliation.

The postbellum period, however, brought a different kind of change. Black men briefly attained political power but the withdrawal of federal troops from the South in 1877 undercut the promise of Radical Reconstruction. The rise of white redemption, compounded by the Supreme Court's reversal of the Civil Rights Act of 1875, undermined black hopes for equality and freedom. In her study on black women writers, Peterson observes that "[o]ne important consequence of Reconstruction for the black community was a deepening of class and gender divisions that had already made themselves felt before the Civil War."[199] Spotlighting intraracial class and gender distinctions some fifty years later, Nella Larsen's novels highlight elite blacks' economic distance from the masses, while emphasizing black women's complex subjectivity along the axes of race, class, and gender.

NOTES

1. "Address on Colonization to a Deputation of Negroes" in *Lincoln on Race and Slavery*, ed. Henry Louis Gates Jr. and David Yacovone (Princeton: Princeton University Press, 2009), 236.
2. Gates, "Address on Colonization," 235.
3. Gates, "Address on Colonization," 236.
4. Gates, "Address on Colonization," 237.
5. Charles H. Wesley, "Lincoln's Plan for Colonizing the Emancipated Negroes," *Journal of Negro History*, 4 (1919): 7–21; see pages 15–20.
6. Gates, "Address on Colonization," 235.
7. Gates, "Address on Colonization," 235–36.
8. Introduction to *The Curse of Caste; or The Slave Bride: A Rediscovered African American Novel* by Julia C. Collins, ed. William L. Andrews and Mitch Kachun (New York: Oxford University Press, 2006), xxi.
9. Qtd. In Introduction, Andrews and Kachun, *The Curse of Caste*, xvi.
10. Qtd. In Introduction, Andrews and Kachun, *The Curse of Caste*, xvi.
11. Qtd. In Introduction, Andrews and Kachun, *The Curse of Caste*, xvi.
12. George Lipsitz, *The Possessive Investment in Whiteness: How White People Profit from Identity Politics* (Philadelphia: Temple University Press, 1998), vii.
13. Charles W. Mills, *The Racial Contract* (Ithaca: Cornell University Press, 1997), 13–14.
14. Mills, *The Racial Contract*, 20.
15. Mills, *The Racial Contract*, 30.
16. Mills, *The Racial Contract*, 30.

17. Qtd. in David Levering Lewis, *W. E. B. Du Bois, 1919–1963: The Fight for Equality and the American Century* (New York: Henry Holt and Company, 2000), 371.
18. Collins, *The Curse of Caste*, 129.
19. Collins, *The Curse of Caste*, 132.
20. See George Yancy, *Look, A White!: Philosophical Essays on Whiteness* (Philadelphia: Temple University Press, 2012), 140.
21. Julia Collins died before drafting (or perhaps submitting) the final chapter of her novel, so her incomplete work has given way to much speculation about her authorial goals.
22. Mitch Kachun, "Interrogating the Silences: Julia C. Collins, 19th-Century Black Readers and Writers, and the *Christian Recorder*," *African American Review*, 40 (2006): 652.
23. For a detailed discussion of the *Christian Recorder*'s subscribers, see Eric Gardner, *Black Print Unbound: The Christian Recorder, African American Literature, and Periodical Culture* (New York: Oxford University Press, 2015), 115.
24. Kachun asserts, "[w]hites associated with African American regiments also 'read the Recorder with great interest' (Johnson)." See Kachun, "Interrogating the Silences," 652.
25. Frances Smith Foster and Chanta Haywood, "Christian Recordings: Afro-Protestantism, Its Press, and the Production of African-American Literature," *Religion and Literature*, 27 (1995): 24.
26. Carla Peterson, *"Doers of the Word": African-American Women Speakers and Writers in the North, 1830–1880* (New York: Oxford University Press, 1995), 235.
27. Foster and Haywood, "Christian Recordings," 31.
28. Kachun, "Interrogating the Silences," 652.
29. See, for example, Andrews and Kachun, 2006; and Tomeiko Ashford Carter, "The Sentiment of the Christian Serial Novel: *The Curse of Caste; or the Slave Bride* and the AME *Christian Recorder*," *African American Review*, 40 (2006): 717–30.
30. bell hooks, *All About Love: New Visions* (New York: Perennial, 2000), 5.
31. Bertram Wyatt-Brown, *Southern Honor: Ethics and Behavior in the Old South* (New York: Oxford University Press, 1982), 4.
32. Wyatt-Brown, *Southern Honor*, 14.
33. Wyatt-Brown, *Southern Honor*, 3.
34. Wyatt-Brown, *Southern Honor*, 4.
35. Collins, *The Curse of Caste*, 39.
36. Collins, *The Curse of Caste*, 21.
37. Collins, *The Curse of Caste*, 40, emphasis mine.
38. Collins, *The Curse of Caste*, 40, emphasis mine.
39. Collins, *The Curse of Caste*, 40. Attentive to black female sexuality, the narrative also disrupts dehumanizing representations of hypersexual black women, such that Richard rejects his father's dismissal of Lina as an "artful wench," a stereotypical black female seductress, insisting instead on her "purity."
40. Collins, *The Curse of Caste*, 42.
41. See Robert E. Birt, "The Bad Faith of Whiteness" in *What White Looks Like: African-American Philosophers on the Whiteness Question*, ed. George Yancy (New York: Routledge, 2004), 55–64. Quote appears on page 58.
42. Birt, "The Bad Faith of Whiteness," 58.
43. Birt, "The Bad Faith of Whiteness," 57.
44. Mills, *The Racial Contract*, 19, original emphasis.
45. Mills, *The Racial Contract*, 14.
46. Collins, *The Curse of Caste*, 41.
47. Wolfgang Iser, "The Reading Process: A Phenomenological Approach" in *Reader-Response Criticism: From Formalism to Post-Structuralism*, ed. Jane P. Tompkins (Baltimore: The Johns Hopkins University Press, 1980), 65.
48. Collins, *The Curse of Caste*, 14.
49. Collins, *The Curse of Caste*, 29.

50. Collins, *The Curse of Caste*, 54.
51. Collins, *The Curse of Caste*, 25.
52. Qtd. in Virginia Cope, "'I Verily Believed Myself to Be a Free Woman'": Harriet Jacobs's Journey into Capitalism," *African American Review* 38 (2004): 6, xvii.
53. Cope, "'I Verily Believed Myself to be a Free Woman,'" 6.
54. Collins, *The Curse of Caste*, 128
55. Wyatt-Brown, *The Shaping of Southern Culture: Honor, Grace, and War, 1760s–1880s* (Chapel Hill: The University of North Carolina Press, 2001), 57.
56. Collins, *The Curse of Caste*, 30
57. Collins, *The Curse of Caste*, 56.
58. Wyatt-Brown, *Southern Honor*, 34. Also, on the colonel and the problem of republican citizenship, see Colleen C. O'Brien, "What the Dickens? Intertexual Influence and the Inheritance of Virtue in Julia C. Collins's *The Curse of Caste; or the Slave Bride*," *African American Review*, 40 (2006): 661–85.
59. Collins, *The Curse of Caste*, 60.
60. Collins, *The Curse of Caste*, 21.
61. Wyatt-Brown, *Southern Honor*, 45.
62. Collins, *The Curse of Caste*, 21.
63. Collins, *The Curse of Caste*, 40.
64. James Oliver Horton and Lois E. Horton, *Slavery and the Making of America* (New York: Oxford University Press, 2005), 109
65. Harriet Jacobs, *Incidents in the Life of a Slave Girl*, 1861. Electronic edition, http://docsouth.unc.edu/fpn/jacobs/jacobs.html, accessed January 17, 2017.
66. Collins, *The Curse of Caste*, 58.
67. Collins, *The Curse of Caste*, 57.
68. Collins, *The Curse of Caste*, 58.
69. Collins, *The Curse of Caste*, 61.
70. Collins, *The Curse of Caste*, 59.
71. Collins, *The Curse of Caste*, 58.
72. Collins, *The Curse of Caste*, 132.
73. Collins, *The Curse of Caste*, 59.
74. Collins, *The Curse of Caste*, 59.
75. Collins, *The Curse of Caste*, 58.
76. Wyatt-Brown, *Southern Honor*, 22.
77. Collins, *The Curse of Caste*, 59, original emphasis.
78. Collins, *The Curse of Caste*, 59.
79. Collins, *The Curse of Caste*, 58.
80. Collins, *The Curse of Caste*, 58.
81. Qtd. in hooks, *All About Love: New Visions* (New York: Perennial, 2000), 4. Here, hooks draws on M. Scott Peck's definition of love.
82. Silvan Tomkins, *Shame and Its Sisters: A Silvan Tomkins Reader*, ed. Eve Sedgwick and Adam Frank (Durham: Duke University Press, 1995), 119.
83. Tomkins, *Shame and Its Sisters*, 111.
84. Tomkins, *Shame and Its Sisters*, 120.
85. Iser, "The Reading Process," 65.
86. Collins, *The Curse of Caste*, 5.
87. Collins, *The Curse of Caste*, 5.
88. Veta Tucker, "A Tale of Disunion: The Racial Politics of Unclaimed Kindred in Julia C. Collins's *The Curse of Caste; or the Slave Bride*," *African American Review*, 40 (2006): 744.
89. Tucker, "A Tale of Disunion," 744.
90. Collins, *The Curse of Caste*, 6.
91. Andrea N. Williams, "African American Literary Realism, 1865–1914" in *A Companion to African American Literature*, ed. Gene Andrew Jarrett (Malden: Wiley-Blackwell, 2010), 192.

92. Jane Tompkins, Introduction to *Sensational Designs: The Cultural Work of American Fiction, 1790–1860* (New York: Oxford University Press, 1985), xi.
93. Tompkins, Introduction, xi.
94. James Chandler, *An Archaeology of Sympathy: The Sentimental Mode in Literature and Cinema* (Chicago: The University of Chicago Press, 2013), xvii.
95. Elizabeth Barnes, "Affecting Relations: Pedagogy, Patriarchy, and the Politics of Sympathy," *American Literary History*, 8 (1996): 600.
96. Barnes, "Affecting Relations," 597.
97. Barnes, "Affecting Relations," 603.
98. Barnes, "Affecting Relations," 607.
99. Barnes, "Affecting Relations," 597.
100. Here, I draw on Barnes's characterization of William Hill Brown's *The Power of Sympathy*, which "represents sympathetic attachment in its story line" and "reproduce[s] it in the relationship between reader and text," 597.
101. Qtd. in Lindsay B. Cummings, "Naomi Wallace and the Dramaturgy of Rehearsal" in *The Theatre of Naomi Wallace: Embodied Dialogues*, ed. Scott Cummings and Erica Stevens Abbitt (New York: Palgrave Macmillan, 2013), 75.
102. Cummings, "Naomi Wallace," 75.
103. Martha Nussbaum, "Compassion: The Basic Social Emotion," *Social Philosophy and Policy* 13 (1996): 27–58. Quote appears on page 29.
104. Martha Nussbaum, "Can Patriotism Be Compassionate? Moral concern begins with the local, but shouldn't stop there." *The Nation*, November 29, 2001, accessed January 17, 2017.
105. Nussbaum, "Compassion," 51.
106. Nussbaum, "Compassion," 51.
107. Laura Wexler, "Tender Violence: Literary Eavesdropping, Domestic Fiction, and Educational Reform" in *The Culture of Sentiment: Race, Gender, and Sentimentality in Nineteenth-Century America*, ed. Shirley Samuels. (New York: Oxford University Press, 1992), 17.
108. Laura Wexler, "Tender Violence," 17–18.
109. See Saidiya Hartman, *Scenes of Subjection: Terror, Slavery, and Self-Making in Nineteenth-Century America* (New York: Oxford University Press, 1997).
110. Collins, *The Curse of Caste*, 9.
111. Collins, *The Curse of Caste*, 4.
112. Sara Ahmed, "Happy Objects" in *The Affect Theory Reader*, ed. Melissa Gregg and Gregory J. Seigworth (Durham: Duke University Press, 2010), 29–51. Quote appears on page 31.
113. Locke, Qtd. in Ahmed, "Happy Objects," 31.
114. Collins, *The Curse of Caste*, 8.
115. Collins, The *Curse of Caste*, 131.
116. Collins, The *Curse of Caste*, 9.
117. Collins, *The Curse of Caste*, 10.
118. Collins, *The Curse of Caste*, 31.
119. Collins, *The Curse of Caste*, 35.
120. Gardner, *Black Print Unbound*, 246.
121. Gardner, *Black Print Unbound*, 246
122. Joanne Dobson, "Reclaiming Sentimental Literature," *American Literature: A Journal of Literary History, Criticism, and Bibliography*, 69 (1997): 267.
123. Collins, *The Curse of Caste*, 5.
124. Collins, *The Curse of Caste*, 10.
125. Collins, *The Curse of Caste*, 10.
126. Collins, *The Curse of Caste*, 89, emphasis mine.
127. Collins, *The Curse of Caste*, 89.
128. *Friendship, A History*, ed. Barbara Caine (New York: Routledge, 2014), 22.
129. Caine, *Friendship*, 22.
130. Qtd. in Caine, *Friendship*, 23.

131. Heather Williams, *Help Me to Find My People: The African American Search for Family Lost in Slavery* (Chapel Hill: The University of North Carolina Press, 2012), 153.
132. Williams, *Help Me to Find My People*, 153.
133. Williams, *Help Me to Find My People*, 159.
134. Jean Lee Cole, "Information Wanted: The Curse of Caste, Minnie's Sacrifice, and the *Christian Recorder*," *African American Review*, 40 (2006): 731.
135. Cole, "Information Wanted," 737.
136. Collins, *The Curse of Caste*, 12.
137. Gardner, *Black Print Unbound*, 237.
138. Gardner, *Black Print Unbound*, 238.
139. Qtd. in Melissa V. Harris-Perry, *Sister Citizen: Shame, Stereotypes, and Black Women in America* (New Haven: Yale University Press, 2011), 77.
140. Collins, *The Curse of Caste*, 89.
141. Collins, *The Curse of Caste*, 89. As Gardner points out, the narrator addresses Juno as "unsophisticated" which suggests "Juno does carry some of the 'stock character' traits" addressed in his study. See *Black Print Unbound*, 244.
142. Collins, *The Curse of Caste*, 89.
143. Jennifer Rae Greeson, "'Ruse It Well': Reading, Power, and the Seduction Plot in *The Curse of Caste*," *African American Review*, 40 (2006): 774.
144. Andrews and Kachun, introduction to *The Curse of Caste*, xii.
145. Collins, *The Curse of Caste*, 87.
146. Ahmed, "Happy Objects," 31.
147. Ahmed, "Happy Objects," 33.
148. Collins, *The Curse of Caste*, 87.
149. Collins, *The Curse of Caste*, 87.
150. Samuels, introduction to *The Culture of Sentiment*, 3.
151. Collins, *The Curse of Caste*, 86.
152. Collins, *The Curse of Caste*, 103.
153. Collins, *The Curse of Caste*, 103.
154. Collins, *The Curse of Caste*, 76.
155. Collins, *The Curse of Caste*, 103.
156. Here, hooks draws on Scott Peck's definition of love, inspired by Erich Fromm. See *All About Love*, 4.
157. Collins, *The Curse of Caste*, 87.
158. See Gardner, *Black Print Unbound*. See also Tomeiko Ashford Carter, "The Sentiment of the Christian Serial Novel: *The Curse of Caste; or the Slave* Bride and the AME *Christian Recorder*," *African American Review*, 40 (2006): 717–30.
159. Gardner, *Black Print Unbound*, 248.
160. Carter, "The Sentiment of the Christian Serial Novel," 720.
161. Collins, *The Curse of Caste*, 80.
162. Collins, *The Curse of Caste*, 57.
163. Collins, *The Curse of Caste*, 55.
164. Collins, *The Curse of Caste*, 21.
165. Collins, *The Curse of Caste*, 108.
166. Pope John Paul, "Apostolic Letter of John Paul II: On the Christian Meaning of Human Suffering," https://www.ewtn.com/library/papaldoc/jp2salvi.htm, accessed January 17, 2017.
167. Collins, *The Curse of Caste*, 58, 59.
168. Collins, *The Curse of Caste*, 64.
169. Collins, *The Curse of Caste*, 103.
170. Collins, *The Curse of Caste*, 107.
171. Collins, *The Curse of Caste*, 99.
172. Collins, *The Curse of Caste*, 103.
173. Collins, *The Curse of Caste*, 43.
174. Collins, *The Curse of Caste*, 44.
175. Collins, *The Curse of Caste*, 44.

176. Martha Nussbaum, "Can Patriotism Be Compassionate? Moral concern begins with the local, but shouldn't stop there," *The Nation*, November 29, 2001, accessed January 17, 2017.
177. Collins, *The Curse of Caste*, 44.
178. Joycelyn Moody, *Sentimental Confessions: Spiritual Narratives of Nineteenth-Century African American Women* (Athens: The University of Georgia Press, 2003), 9.
179. Moody, *Sentimental Confessions*, 15.
180. Moody, *Sentimental Confessions*, 8.
181. For a complete discussion of this dynamic, see Veta Tucker, "A Tale of Disunion," 743.
182. Collins, *The Curse of Caste*, 125.
183. Collins, *The Curse of Caste*, 88.
184. Collins, *The Curse of Caste*, 89.
185. Collins, *The Curse of Caste*, 23.
186. Collins, *The Curse of Caste*, 22.
187. Collins, *The Curse of Caste*, 37.
188. Collins, *The Curse of Caste*, 13.
189. For a compelling discussion of Claire's role as teacher, see Gabrielle P. Foreman, "The *Christian Recorder*, Broken Families, and Educated Nations in Julia C. Collins's Civil War Novel *The Curse of Caste*," *African American Review*, 40 (2006): 705–16.
190. Collins, *The Curse of Caste*, 85.
191. Collins, *The Curse of Caste*, 87.
192. Tucker, "A Tale of Disunion," 744.
193. See Kevin Gaines, *Uplifting the Race: Black Leadership, Politics, and Culture in the Twentieth Century* (Chapel Hill: University of North Carolina Press, 1996).
194. bell hooks, *Outlaw Culture: Resisting Representations* (New York: Routledge, 1994), 290.
195. hooks, *Outlaw Culture*, 290.
196. Collins, *The Curse of Caste*, 111.
197. Collins, *The Curse of Caste*, 32, 49. In "Happy Objects," Ahmed "explores how the family sustains its place as a 'happy object' by identifying those who do not reproduce its line as the cause of unhappiness," 30. She takes *Bend It Like Beckham* as her textual object but I find her approach useful in analyzing Claire's relation to her long-lost "family."
198. Gabrielle P. Foreman, "The *Christian Recorder*, Broken Families, and Educated Nations," 711.
199. Peterson, *Doers of the Word*, 198.

THREE
Nella Larsen's Spiritual Strivings

Love figures prominently in Harper's "The Two Offers" (1859) and Collins's *The Curse of Caste,* but its elusiveness in Nella Larsen's novels reveals broad sociopolitical problems plaguing the modern world. A critically acclaimed author, Larsen published two articles for children, two novels, and three short stories during her brief literary career. *Quicksand* (1928) earned enthusiastic praise from Harlem Renaissance writer W. E. B. Du Bois who hailed it as "the best piece of fiction that Negro America has produced since the heyday of Chesnutt."[1] Her second novel *Passing* (1929) garnered its share of favorable and lukewarm reviews in the white press, but elicited another warm endorsement from Du Bois, who praised it as "one of the finest novels of the year."[2] Though widely celebrated during the renaissance by such luminaries as Du Bois, James Weldon Johnson, Walter White, and Carl Van Vechten, and honored with a Guggenheim award in 1930, her literary works had virtually disappeared from view by 1986, when Deborah McDowell reissued her short novels in a collected volume. The so-called "mystery woman" of the renaissance,[3] Larsen "was one of several women writers of the Harlem Renaissance relegated to the back pages of the movement's literary history."[4]

In recent years, black feminist theory, queer theory, performance studies, as well as studies in visual culture and psychoanalysis have offered rich insights and constructive interpretive lenses for Larsen scholars. Early moves in Larsen criticism primarily explore the author's treatment of the mulatta figure and assert her underdeveloped black subjectivity in Larsen's novels. Most notably, Nathan Huggins laments the problem of the "mulatto condition" in Larsen's fiction and reads these works as political failures.[5] Hiroko Sato notes that Larsen uses "a very particular situation of mixed blood" in *Quicksand* to express a "tragic situation,"[6] while Barbara Christian argues that in *Quicksand* "the tragic mulattas of the abolitionist novels finally reach bitter fruition."[7] Connecting the dots between Larsen's biography and her fiction, Christian asserts that "Larsen's novels, as well as her life, are the quintessence of the tragic mulatta image."[8] Born to a black West Indian father and a Danish mother, Larsen fictionalized and incorporated into her fiction selected biographical details.[9] But her novels exceed mere biography, revealing broad imaginative power and astute literary skill.

The history of scholarship on Nella Larsen's novels illuminates the rich tensions and textures structuring her fiction: the alluring aesthetics, modern style, and multifaceted themes mark *Quicksand* and *Passing* as penetrating works of artistic genius. While a considerable body of vibrant scholarship examines how the "matrix of domination" impacts the psyche and material realities of Larsen's light-skinned African American heroines,[10] comparatively little has been written about Helga Crane's and Irene Redfield's encounters with the spiritual sterility plaguing their barren lives. Religion figures prominently in *Quicksand* and less so in *Passing* yet its signifying presence in both texts yields rich insight into black women's complex spiritual and psychological negotiations in the modern world. This critical analysis will show that Helga's spiritual search, and subsequent merging with a "white" God, can be read fruitfully alongside Irene's perfunctory prayers and efforts to "play god" within the domestic sphere. Silvan Tomkins and Teresa Brennan offer useful frameworks for analyzing negative affects to shed further light on Helga's and Irene's gendered and racialized plight in the modern world. Interestingly, these women's spiritual journeys reveal a despair and soul sickness that cannot be "fixed" by "[t]hings. Things. Things."[11]

CRITICAL HISTORY: *QUICKSAND* AND *PASSING*

A brief review of key scholarship on Larsen's novels contextualizes my claims about her protagonists' subjectivity and spirituality. Simply put, critics have argued over how *Quicksand* and *Passing* ought to be read. Attentive psychological readings of the novel, for example, emend criticism confining Larsen's heroines to the fate of the tragic mulatta. Nineteenth-century abolitionist narratives and antislavery fiction frequently feature near-white heroines who find themselves caught tragically between black and white worlds. It was generally assumed by earlier critics like Barbara Christian, that African American authors highlighted fair-skinned victims of slavery to evoke white sympathy and resist black stereotypes. But as Hazel Carby has shown, the mulatta figure also serves as a literary device for exploring one of the most controversial and taboo topics in the nineteenth century. The mulatta figure is not merely a concession to white literary tastes but may also be read as "a vehicle for an exploration of the relationship between the races, and, at the same time, an expression of the relationship between the races."[12]

Writing in the early twentieth century, Larsen clearly evokes the tragic mulatta trope in *Quicksand* in the epigraph from Langston Hughes' poem "Cross," which voices the mixed-raced speaker's anxiety about racial belonging. But as McDowell correctly argues, Larsen's concerns span beyond this dominant fictional icon.[13] In her view, "the contradictory impulses of Larsen's novels are clear in the psychic divisions of her characters, divisions especially apparent in Helga Crane of *Quicksand*."[14] Rather than falling victim to the "confusion" that "mixed racial heritage creates," McDowell asserts that Helga "is divided psychically between a desire for sexual fulfillment and a longing for social respectability."[15]

McDowell emphasizes Helga's "sexual desires,"[16] while Cheryl A. Wall's psychological reading is more attentive to issues of race and asserts that Larsen's novels reveal "the psychological costs of racism and sexism."[17] Rather than understanding Helga primarily in sexual terms, Wall writes that *Quicksand* and *Passing* are meditations on the "inextricability of the racism and sexism that confront the black woman in her quest for a wholly integrated identity."[18] She contends that Helga must resist white "fantasies of the exotic female Other" on the one hand,[19] and restrictive black "male definitions of womanhood" on the other.[20] That is, she describes Helga's bifurcated dilemma as one in which Helga fights against white assumptions that blacks are savage, primitive beings, even as she feels "trapped by the need to repress her sexuality, and to assume the ornamental, acquiescent role of 'lady'" embraced by middle-class blacks.[21]

Expanding upon early Larsen scholarship, recent cultural critics take a variety of innovative approaches to *Quicksand*. Drawing on visual culture, and contributing to scholarship on the iconography of the mulatta figure, critic Cherene Sherrard-Johnson argues persuasively for a "painterly rather than writerly reading of Larsen's work."[22] She asserts that in "Larsen's search for a transgressive, transcendent heroine, her tableaux revise the black female subject in modernist works of art and popular visual culture—in effect, modernizing the mulatta figure"[23] Clearly, Helga Crane is a "modern alienated individual" who experiences the anxieties and insecurities generated by baffling changes and uncontrollable forces in the modern world.[24] That Helga turns to religion to negotiate her fears is occasionally remarked upon by critics but, as I argue below, Helga's spiritual experience warrants further attention for it reveals much about the spiritual condition of black women at the turn of the century.

Like *Quicksand*, Larsen's second novel, *Passing*, studies a sophisticated black woman in the modern world who engages religion to assuage her fears. Understandably, however, one of the primary concerns for literary critics has been Larsen's treatment of racial "passing." Early critics, namely Robert Bone and Sterling Brown, explore passing exclusively through the figure of Clare. According to Bone, who ignores Irene's habit of strategic passing, "the invariable outcome" in the passing novel "is disillusionment with life on the other side of the line" and a "new appreciation of racial values."[25] Also figuring Clare as the lone passer, Brown reads her as the tragic mulatta who falls to her death[26]; conversely Mary Mabel Youman characterizes Irene as the ultimate passer noting that although she "remains 'Black,'" Irene has in fact "sold her soul and 'passed' into white inhumanity."[27] Late-twentieth- and early-twenty-first-century critics such as Lauren Berlant, Martha Cutter, Catherine Rottenberg, and Sherrard-Johnson—largely influenced by poststructuralist theory—refuse racially essentialist readings linking values to phenotype.[28] Broader trends in black feminist theory, poststructuralist theory, and performance studies inflect recent scholarship on *Passing* and help elucidate the nuanced sites of cultural disruption and protest shaping Larsen's novel.

DIVINE CONNECTIONS:
THE QUEST FOR GOD IN LARSEN'S FICTION

Adding to the rich critical history of Larsen scholarship, I argue that Helga's and Irene's spiritually sterile lives, and their likely deaths (literal in *Quicksand* and metaphorical in *Passing*) can be read as critiques not only of bourgeois values but also as critiques of restrictive religiosity and vacuous religious ritual detached from critical self-reflection. Elizabeth West rightly notes that, in *Quicksand*, Larsen suggests that "while blacks still seek spiritual enlightenment and deliverance in the church, the church cannot answer their needs because it is little more than a tool of white exploitation."[29] Indeed, Western constructions of Christianity prove to be restrictive for black women in Larsen's novels. But much remains to be said about Helga's and Irene's unreflective and uncritical engagement with religion, and Larsen's critique of them. Further, Larsen's novels present a study of how middle-class black women mired in oppressive systems of race and gender negotiate their own powerlessness and strive to become spiritually fulfilled agents. My focus on their shame, distress, and fear further shows how negative affects motivate Helga's and Irene's fraught relations in the modern world.

Remarkable not only for its literary skill, *Quicksand* wrestles poignantly with the complexities of being black in the industrial capital age. Specifically, despite her education, talent, and beauty, Helga has a problem. She flees Naxos for Chicago, abandons Chicago for Harlem, and Harlem for Denmark; but happiness eludes her. Helga returns to Harlem in the second half of the novel, only to again change her locale to a rural southern town. But what drives Helga's decisions, and disturbs her so? Why can she not find happiness while other black women are able to do so?

Many critics locate the cause of Helga's troubles in her biracial identity and/or her unhappy childhood, when she endured "the savage unkindness of her stepbrothers and sisters, and the jealous, malicious hatred of her mother's [white] husband."[30] In his racial reading of Helga's plight, Huggins argues that "Helga Crane is overwhelmed by the ethnic war within her mulatto psyche."[31] Wall, on the other hand, argues the "primary cause" of Helga's "unease" is not her interracial parentage and mixed blood but rather "the imposed definitions of blackness and womanhood" and her "inability to define alternatives."[32] Charles Larson asserts that, as a "dark child," Helga was "psychologically if not physically abused."[33]

Several critics cite parental rejection and racial insecurity as causes for Helga's despair, but they disagree on why she cannot overcome these difficult formative years.[34] Concerned with Helga's "divided" and "disintegrating self," Thadious Davis writes she "can find no viable outlet for her aesthetic concerns" due to complexities of race and gender.[35] Following Davis, Jacquelyn Y. McLendon argues that Helga's "struggle is against a conventional, unimaginative society that suppresses individualism"; her real self is therefore "trapped" within social constructions.[36] Conversely, Cutter argues that "Helga repeatedly attempts to find a true identity, only to learn that no such thing exists, only a variety of social roles."[37] More recently Sherrard-Johnson, exploring Helga's artistic aspirations, finds that Helga's "potential for artistic or intellectual production is subsumed beneath the reproductive duties of a wife." Ultimately, she argues, "*Quicksand's* tableaux turn the tragic aspect of the mulatta trope into the frustration of black female artists and intellectuals."[38]

Drawing on affect studies to illuminate Helga's state, Sianne Ngai analyzes Helga's often illegible response to myriad social stimuli. Focusing on "the negative affects," Ngai asserts that "Larsen's novel prefers the 'superficial' affect of irritation—a conspicuously weak or inadequate form of anger." Ultimately, writes Ngai, "the novel's irritated aesthetic enables us to continue the exploration of the ideologically fraught relationship between emotion, race, and aesthetics as it comes to a head in the context of the Harlem Renaissance."[39]

Expanding on the critical work of these important scholars, I investigate how black women have managed the "frustration" that Sherrard-Johnson identifies and negotiated the "irritation" that Ngai illumines, and argue for a reconsideration of religion and the spirituality in Larsen's novels. In particular, I examine how the black heroines strive to become spiritually empowered agents in the modern world. In *Quicksand*, Helga Crane's search for fulfillment in a variety of jobs and locales proves fruitless. When she returns to Harlem she gets "saved" but her subsequent longed-for spiritual peace dissipates, leaving her empty and despairing of God's existence. In *Passing* Irene also seeks divine aid, with little success. Equating marriage with emotional security, Irene desperately wields "god-like" power on the domestic front so that she can quell her husband Brian's restless desire to abandon both his racial uplift work, and America altogether. Realizing the limits of her personal power, Irene prays to a distant God and dabbles in religious discourse in her search for inner peace. But these efforts to play god and appeal to God do not bring her security. For both Helga and Irene, there is a "lack somewhere."[40]

A number of critics have examined Helga's brief and dispiriting foray into the religious realm. Her conversion, the effects of which are short-lived, occurs after Dr. Anderson's rejection drives her to a state of humiliating despair. Unable to accept the knowledge that Dr. Anderson knows of her desire for him but refuses to satisfy it, Helga wanders out of her Harlem hotel room one night into the cold rain, walking aimlessly about until she falls into a gutter. Wet and exhausted, she approaches a light illuminating what turns out to be a black storefront church. Critics have variously interpreted the conversion scene that follows as "credible,"[41] resembling a "typical service" at a fundamentalist church,[42] and suggestive of "gang rape."[43] Significantly, the narrative voice marks Helga's religious experience as the moment in which she "was lost — or saved."[44] The narrator's ambivalence here telegraphs Helga's journey on the religious path because in becoming "saved," she loses — or more specifically — relinquishes her reasoning self to a Western, patriarchal God concept.

Helga temporarily abandons critical thinking and seeks refuge from reality in her faith after she sleeps with the Reverend Pleasant Green, whom she marries "in the confusion of seductive repentance."[45] She does not love him but she does "initially accep[t]" the social script that marriage makes sex moral in the eyes of the law and the church."[46] Changing her locale to rural Alabama, where her husband pastors a "primitive flock," Helga assures herself that she "believes in her religion" precisely "[b]ecause in its coming it had brought this other thing, the anaesthetic satisfaction for her senses."[47] A socially disengaged Christian, Helga uses her religion to dull her senses and withdraw into an idyllic inner world. Rather than facing honestly her impoverished status in the rural South, Helga comforts herself with the platitude that "life was utterly filled with the glory and the marvel of God."[48] In reality it consists of dull, strenuous housework.[49] Lulled into a deluded state that "color[s] all her thoughts and acts," Helga casts a romantic light on her ugly house to avoid reconciling herself to the "nakedness of its uncovered painted floors."[50] Religion offers her an escape hatch so that she can hide from the horrors of poverty, the unpleasantness of her unhygienic husband, and the exhaustion of domestic labor.

Helga's marriage exemplifies the negative features of patriarchy, as it manifests itself both in religion and marriage. Ill in body and broken in spirit after birthing three children in twenty months,[51] Helga appeals for support to the reverend, who "had lost any personal interest in her, except for the short spaces between the times when she was preparing for or recovering from childbirth."[52] Brushing away her doubts about her ability to cope with yet another child, the reverend counsels, "[we] must accept what God sends,"[53] and advises that she "trust the Lord more fully."[54] As pastor and representative of the church, Green manipulates religious platitudes to secure his position of power, and reinforce Helga's subordinate position as wife and mother. As many critics have suggested, Larsen's depiction of the relationship between Helga and Pleasant Green critiques the patriarchal forces underlying the institution of marriage.[55] Diminishing his wife's fears about her physical frailty, Pleasant Green assures Helga that her condition "was a natural thing, an act of God."[56] Functioning as a transparency for God, the reverend proclaims that Helga's suffering is God-ordained and thus natural. His disturbing logic resonates with the sermons of proslavery preachers who once counseled slaves to obey their masters.

When Helga approaches her female neighbors for domestic guidance and emotional support she fares no better. They respond with "an upward rolling of eyeballs with a mention of 'de Lawd' looking after us all."[57] According to neighbor Sary Jones, "In de nex'worl' we's all recompense."[58] Like the reverend, Helga's neighbors espouse platitudes reinforcing the subordinate position of poor, black rural women. As Carby indicates, "Larsen's representation of the folk was as the deluded."[59] *Quicksand* thus emphasizes the social blindness produced by culturally dominant and patriarchal theological paradigms, as religious dogma prevents Sary and her peers from analyzing critically the broader socioeconomic forces that oppress them and perpetuate their poverty. While critics have given some attention to the role of religion in *Quicksand*, much remains to be said about Helga's blinding, faith-filled theology, and her problematic passivity in the face of injustice. More specifically, Helga strives by any means necessary to soothe her spiritual hunger. While her encounter with the sacred reveals how restrictive religious ideology serves to oppress women in marriage and to exploit the poor whose subordinate subject position gets interpreted as part of God's plan, the fact of Helga's hunger permeates the novel and raises additional questions about black middle-class identity in the modern world.

In Denmark, before her Harlem conversion, Helga acknowledges and despises the fundamentally racist nature of the United States. Reflecting, as a black woman, on white supremacy from abroad, Helga recognizes how

> stupid she had been ever to have thought that she could marry and perhaps have children in a land where every dark child was handicapped at the start by the shroud of color! She saw, suddenly, the giving birth to little, helpless, unprotesting Negro children as a sin....

More black folks to suffer indignities. More dark bodies for mobs to lynch.[60]

Gazing from Europe on the specter of American racism disturbs and provokes Helga, who responds viscerally to the indignities suffered by black citizens. She does not "think often of America" because black lived experience in the states is "too disturbing" for her.[61] But in the passage above she dwells on the humiliations heaped on blacks, and berates herself for having assumed that she would contribute to it in any way. Notably, Hegla "turned her back on painful America, resolutely shutting out the griefs, the humiliations, the frustrations, which she had endured there."[62] According to Tomkins, "shame is the affect of indignity" that "strikes deepest into the heart of man" and "is felt as an inner torment."[63] The systemic oppression shaping black life in America and the nation's rejection of its black citizens produce profound shame and disappointment in Helga. Indeed, she views America as a "painful" place causing undue suffering that compels her to remain—at present—in Denmark. Actively refusing in that moment to increase by one soul the black population, Helga views herself as an agent withholding at least one black body from the potential pool of lynch mob victims.

Helga's compulsion to take action, albeit in the form of withholding, contrasts strongly with her benign, post-conversion response to racial injustice in Alabama. Surprisingly, she turns a blind eye to the suffering of "the smallest, dirtiest, brown child, barefooted in the fields or muddy road," romanticizing his existence as "an emblem of the wonder of life, of love, and of God's goodness."[64] Robbed of her critical sensibility, Helga displays a passive faith that toothlessly sentimentalizes human need rather than responding to it. Unlike the activist-heroines in Frances E.W. Harper's "The Two Offers" (1859), *Minnie's Sacrifice* (1869), and *Iola Leroy* (1892), Helga's religion sedates but does not inspire her to enact sociopolitical change. Jeanette (as discussed in chapter 1), Minnie, and Iola are faith-filled characters but they do not jettison their reasoning faculties at the door of religion. On the contrary, Jeanette applies her religiosity to gritty antislavery activism, while Minnie's and Iola's religious values empower them to educate and "uplift" the poor in the post-Civil War South. Theologian James Cone argues:

> Black faith emerged out of black people's wrestling with suffering, the struggle to make sense out of their senseless situation, as they related their own predicament to similar stories in the Bible. On the one hand, faith spoke to their suffering, making it bearable, while, on the other hand, suffering contradicted their faith, making it unbearable. That is the profound paradox inherent in black faith, the dialectic of doubt and trust in the search for meaning, as blacks "walked through the valley of the shadow of death."[65]

Clearly, Helga's unquestioning faith makes her suffering "bearable." Yet she refuses to struggle with pain and wrestle with doubt. Opting out of the dialectic that could produce a mature faith born of suffering, Helga instead silences her doubts, allowing religion to shield "her from the cruel light of an unbearable reality."[66] She therefore engages in a superficial religious exercise as her unthinking faith rests on hollow, hegemonic platitudes.

Lackey correctly asserts that Larsen criticizes "the role the God concept plays in the construction of race and gender subordinates and in the construction and definition of the natural."[67] But I would qualify his claim that "[a]s long as theological representation remains intact, certain groups of people will inevitably be subjected to an inferior state of being, so to create the conditions for a healthier and more just body politic, killing God and the idea of nature, whether it is a human's nature or a woman's nature, is a psychological and emotional must."[68] Clearly, *Quicksand* rejects restrictive conceptions of God that would denigrate women and minorities. In this sense Larsen's narrative kills the racist construction of a white and, I would add, sexist God by exposing the material consequences of racist and sexist theology. However the narrative does not depict religion as *fundamentally* corrupt and oppressive. Arguably, its searing critique is specific to racist and sexist discourse that some Christians espouse, and to the socially debilitating theology that Helga internalizes. While the novel expresses the ways religion can become complicit with racism and sexism, at the same time, by doing so, it reveals the importance of constructing a more humane and self-critical theology.

While the novel mocks restrictive religious discourse, it simultaneously emphasizes Helga's spiritual hunger and isolation in the modern world. Before heading to Denmark, Helga is "[h]orribly lonely" in Chicago and therefore visits the Negro Episcopal Church. Although she does not display at this point in the novel an interest in the sacred realm, Helga nonetheless wishes "some good Christian would speak to her, invite her to return, or inquire kindly if she was a stranger in the city."[69] Helga's "uninterested manner adopted . . . as a protective measure" repels potential allies, but she nonetheless makes numerous visits to this church on Sundays.[70] In short, Helga seeks relief from overwhelming distress. In chapter 1, I quote Tomkins, who writes "the vicissitudes of interpersonal relationships"[71] can produce affective distress and that one of the "biological function[s] of crying" is "to motivate both the self and others to do something to reduce the crying response."[72] Larsen's novel captures the distress arising from fluctuating conditions and relationships as Helga arrives in Chicago, where "she had not even any friends," and must search desperately for a job because she cannot obtain money from her Uncle Peter, who is unexpectedly out of town.[73] Indeed, Helga's loneliness had "grown to appalling proportions, encompassing her, shutting her off from all of life around her," and so she was "[d]evastated" and "always on the verge of weeping."[74] A desire to reduce suffering motivates Helga's efforts at outreach that may reveal inner spiritual needs: for human connection, companionship, kindness, and love. Alone in the "mad, hurrying" modern city into which alienated individuals sometimes disappear into anonymous crowds, Helga longs for communion and compassion.[75]

Spiritually empty and alone, Helga struggles to exert agency in the massive city of Chicago. Although she has graduated from Devon and taught at Naxos, Helga cannot easily secure a job in the modern workforce. She "knew books and loved them,"[76] but her work experience has not prepared her to fit into the modern, professionalized slots that require "library training," "library school," and "classification."[77] Race restricts her further, as shops refuse to hire "colored" salespeople and clerks.[78] Plagued by spiritual despair and powerlessness in Chicago, Helga "fe[lt] small and insignificant [because] in all the climbing massed city no one cared a whit about her."[79] Isolated in the large, mystifying city, Helga feels like an outsider looking in. As Meredith Goldsmith argues, Helga purchases items that she cannot afford, "to recuperate the material goods she lacks and the spiritual fulfillment she seeks."[80] Documenting Helga's encounters with burgeoning capitalistic commodity culture, *Quicksand* poignantly captures Helga's materialistic longings and attempts to bolster her self-esteem by accumulating rare and luxurious goods. Goldsmith argues that the "decorative rhetoric that surrounds Helga suggests she, too, is a potential and alluring object of possession. In this tableau, Larsen intimates that Helga's narrative will vacillate between the two poles of woman as consumer and woman as object of consumption."[81] Indeed, Helga consumes even as she comes dangerously close to being consumed. She is "accosted" by a white man on the streets of Chicago who appears to view her as a prostitute,[82] and is also offered money in that city by "a few men, both white and black" for her sexual services during her futile search for work.[83] Further, she is propositioned and later proposed to by painter Axel Olsen, who harbors primitivist ideas about African women but despairs that Helga in particular has been "corrupted by" white civilization and has thus developed "the soul of a prostitute."[84] Helga actively resists such objectification, however, in her refusal of Olsen and her unwillingness to pay the "dear" price for prostituting herself for money.[85] Demonstrating agency and determination, Helga makes plain that she is "not for sale."[86]

Even before she departs for Denmark, Helga encounters racist whites whose prejudice obstructs their ability to "see" her humanity. For example, Helga meets her Uncle Peter's wife—in his absence—when financial need drives her to his home in Chicago. Rather than sympathize with her husband's niece, Mrs. Nilssen rejects her on appearance. Specifically, her racism produces an "atmosphere" and Helga "had felt at once the latent antagonism in the woman's manner."[87] Teresa Brennan, writing on "the transmission of affect" in another context, confirms this process is "social or psychological in origin" and "is also responsible for bodily changes."[88] Provoking this process, Helga's frosty exchange with Mrs. Nilssen, who denies Helga's familial link to her husband and opines that her visit "isn't convenient,"[89] produces unpleasant bodily effects. Helga stammers, feels "pushed down to the uttermost depths of ignominy," and her "lips quivered."[90] Faltering speech and physical oppression index shame and discomfort in the body. But interacting with the unfriendly woman also affects Helga psychologically, stirring up memories of a painful childhood when she had to "discove[r] that because one was dark, one was not necessarily loathsome, and could, therefore, consider oneself without repulsion."[91] In short, her encounter with Mrs. Nilssen revives for the moment prior feelings of racialized self-loathing and Helga thus sees herself from "her mother's, her stepfather's, and his children's points of view": as "an obscene score in all their lives, at all costs to be hidden."[92]

Negotiating a myriad of oppressive socioeconomic forces throughout the narrative, Helga strives to exert agency: she changes her locale to achieve happiness, she decorates herself in fine garments to express her uniqueness, and she terminates romantic relationships when they prove to be unpromising. She "willingly, even eagerly"[93] leaves New York behind after marrying Pleasant Green so that she can maintain her post-conversion "feeling of well-being."[94] Despite these instances of agency, Helga ultimately succumbs to a gloomy fate. Ironically, she engages the sacred realm to escape the pain of alienation—of being "separated even from her own anterior existence"—but her engagement with the divine reinforces her despair.[95] During an extended period of pain and suffering Helga realizes that the "cruel, unrelieved suffering had beaten down her protective wall of artificial faith in the infinite wisdom."[96] No longer cocooned in the platitudes of religion, she determines that God "didn't exist."[97] Deeply embittered, Helga can only dream about "escap[ing] from the oppression" and "think about freedom and cities, and clothes and books."[98] Significantly, she loses her religion but regains her critical sensibility which frees her to dismiss her brand of religion as "'Pie in the sky,'" and to critique her patriarchal marriage as "immoral."[99]

In *Passing* Larsen further explores questions of black female agency and spirituality in the early twentieth century. Protagonist Irene lives a spiritually barren life in plush, middle-class surroundings. Like Helga in her early days, Irene is privileged, insecure, and unhappy. Although Irene possesses an array of material goods, her mind is possessed by the fear that she will lose her husband Brian who longs to leave behind the U.S. and its seething racism. When Brian's "craving for some place strange and different" cropped up early in their marriage, his wife had managed to "repress" it.[100] However it occasionally resurfaces and disturbs Irene, for whom security "was the most important and desired thing in life."[101] Wracked with insecurity, Irene wonders: "Was she never to be free of it, that fear which crouched, always, deep down within her, stealing away the sense of security, the feeling of permanence, from the life which she had so admirably arranged for them all?"[102] Figured as a thief who brazenly occupies a permanent residence in her psyche, fear threatens to destroy Irene's neatly organized life. Living in a perpetual state of anxiety, as divorce could lead to new, unknown terrors, Irene is quite willing to "do anything, risk anything" to get her way.[103] In *The Cultural Politics of Emotion*, Sara Ahmed writes that

> [f]ear, like pain, is felt as an unpleasant form of intensity. But while the lived experience of fear may be unpleasant in the present, the unpleasantness of fear also relates to the future. Fear involves an *anticipation* of hurt or injury. Fear projects us from the present into a future. But the feeling of fear presses us into that future as an intense bodily experience in the present.[104]

Irene knows intimately the terrors of fearful imaginings. She is careful to keep her voice "even" and "her step . . . firm" during volatile exchanges with Brian, but "in her there was no slackening of the agitation, or the alarms, which Brian's expression of discontent had raised."[105] Fearful of the calamity to come, Irene carries in her body a taut "uneasiness" as she tries to "direct and guide her man" toward the future of her choosing.[106]

While Biman Basu argues that Irene "assumes a disciplinary function" in relation to Brian and further delineates her "ascension to managerial power,"[107] I consider the metaphysical implications of Irene's domination of her husband. To compensate for feelings of powerlessness Irene aspires to omnipotence in the domestic sphere. She may want Brian to be happy, but it is "only in her own way and by some *plan of hers for him* that she truly desired him to be so."[108] Irene's all-encompassing "plan" takes on divine proportions, as she tries to manage not only Brian's behavior but also to "*direct for their own best good* the lives of her sons and her husband."[109] Convinced of her own omniscience, Irene presumes to know what is best for her family. Although Brian wants to prepare their sons for the realities of racial discrimination, Irene "won't have it,"[110] as she would protect them from the ugly realities of racism and prolong their childhood innocence. Content that she "belong[s] in this land of rising towers," she decides that Brian does, too.[111] Moreover she determines that his discontent with his job in New York "would die, as long ago she had made up her mind that it should."[112] Believing that declaring a thing makes it so, Irene overestimates her ability to control the outside world, and everyone in it.

Irene fights change because it threatens to disrupt her "fixed, certain" life,[113] and the stability of her middle-class identity. Yet with each passing day Brian grows increasingly remote, and Irene more depressed. Brian's "guarded reserve" is "alarming" because it portends for Irene the failure of her marriage.[114] For all her efforts, Irene despairs that "she, who had prided herself on knowing his moods, their causes and their remedies, had found it first unthinkable, and then intolerable, that this, so like and yet so unlike those other spasmodic restlessnesses of his, should be to her incomprehensible and elusive."[115] Contrasting her former ability to "repress" Brian's discontent with her present inability to detect and eliminate the source of his unhappiness, Irene realizes the limits of her power and the illusory nature of her omnipotence.

Recognizing the finite nature of her power, Irene calls on God for help but her spiritual encounters, much like Helga's, are superficial and unsatisfying. Suspecting Brian and Clare of adultery and struggling to maintain "the outer shell of her marriage,"[116] Irene desperately seeks divine aid to remove Clare, the object of her anxiety.[117] But her vacuous religious ritual, much like her efforts to play god, is yet another attempt to control the outside world without changing herself. Whereas Helga jettisons her will and rational mind to commune with God, Irene relinquishes nothing yet prays for God to do her bidding. To wit, she asks God to "make March come quickly," thereby hastening Clare's departure to Europe and exit from her life.[118] Irene's prayer echoes a long-standing wish as days before she "did wish it were spring, March, so that Clare would be sailing, out of her life and Brian's."[119] She wishes for what she prays, and prays for what she wishes. Significantly, Irene also wishes that "something would only happen" to "remove Claire" from her life.[120] Notably, "as if in answer to her wish" on the following day,[121] Irene encounters on the street Clare's white husband, to whom Irene longs to divulge that his wife "had a touch of the tar-brush" so as to "rid her[self] forever" of her erstwhile friend.[122] The language used to describe the fulfillment of Irene's desire resonates with religious significance because her "answered" wish is an answered prayer. Her wishes slide into prayers and they merge into one. Wishing and praying serve similar functions for Irene: both reflect her desire to quell her anxiety by manipulating others and controlling the course of events. But her self-serving requests, answered though they may be, do not bring the expected peace.

Remarkably, Irene not only prays for God to speed up the calendar, but she also wishes fervently that Clare would die.[123] As if in answer to this wish/prayer, Clare soon enough falls from a window to her death. I agree with Wall and McDowell that Irene is the likely culprit in Clare's demise, as the text strongly supports this reading. Her wish/prayer to eliminate Clare has been answered, and yet her final prayer is not one of gratitude: "'Oh God,' she thought, prayed, 'help me.'"[124] Irene, who has prayed and wished almost unceasingly in the narrative, cannot escape the fundamental insecurity that plagues her psyche.

Rage also rankles Irene, who periodically faces and grapples with racial realities in America. During an informal tea gathering, for instance, Irene meets with John Bellew, who reads her body (along with his wife

Clare's) as white. Unaware of her blackness, Bellew remarks on African Americans: "I don't dislike them, I hate them. . . . They give me the creeps. The black scrimy devils."[125] He further characterizes blacks as "[a]lways robbing and killing people" and "'worse.'"[126] Such reductive, racialist thinking ascribes criminality to blackness and renders whiteness morally innocent. In her analysis of interpersonal relations, Brennan maps the coordinates of racial othering that arguably elucidate Bellew's mindset:

> when I judge the other, I simultaneously direct toward her that negative affect that cuts off my feelings of kinship from her as a fellow living, suffering, joyful creature. . . . The act of directing negative affects to the other severs my kin tie with her by objectifying her. I make her into an object by directing these affects toward her, because that act marks her with affects that I reject in myself.[127]

Similarly, Bellew conflates blackness with badness and irredeemable difference. To him, blacks are not fellow human beings but they are instead inhuman "devils" who produce fear and contempt in law-abiding white citizens like himself. Notably, Bellew's bigotry enrages Irene: during the meeting, she suppresses her "mounting anger and indignation."[128] She feels "rage" but "[o]nly her hands shook slightly."[129] Years later, "the memory of the man's words and manner had power to set her hands to trembling and to send the blood pounding against her temples."[130] While Irene's phenotypic whiteness affords her social privileges and often shields her from overt racism, her interaction with Bellew is instructive and highlights the profound physical impact of racist affect on black bodies. Literally shaken, Irene carries indignation from a two-year-old encounter. At the same time, this scene emphasizes the absence and dire need of love—the care, recognition, and respect that hooks theorizes in her love trilogy[131]—as well as the "loving eye" that Kelly Oliver argues is "always on the lookout for the blind spots that close off the possibility of response-ability and openness to others and difference."[132]

Arguably, Irene cannot imagine herself as an autonomous black female subject as her sense of self is bound up in her identity as wife and mother. She thus "meant to keep [Brian]," though she doubts she loves him.[133] Irene's "race work" as a Negro Welfare League committee member is to her virtually meaningless and more of a habit than a vocation. Her economic privilege and ability to pass separate her from the black masses but within the space of her middle-class world she feels "helpless" because Brian is the key to her "security of place and substance."[134] Irene "fear[s] for the future" that might well include a divorce and the drastic reduction of her social station.[135] As Wall argues, "the absence of meaningful work and community condemn [Larsen's female characters] to the 'walled prison' of their thoughts."[136] But the realities of the racially restrictive job market, as in the previous novel, paint a bleak picture for black women at the turn of the century. According to Paula Giddings, in New York in the early twentieth century, "few women had the resources to enter the professions, and with the discrimination in the semiprofessional and blue-collar occupations, a large number of women had little choice but domestic work."[137] And even those who found work faced "a combination of low-paying jobs and too-high rents [that] often resulted in Blacks' spending more than double the percentage of their income for rent that White families paid."[138]

Seeking refuge from the economic crises beyond the walls of her middle-class home, Irene takes comfort in the stasis of her routine: her tea rituals and her ballroom dances offer temporary comfort but beneath this veneer of security is a frightened soul entrapped in a modern world of few possibilities for the black woman. Brody convincingly argues that the novel's final scene in which Clare is killed is a "biting critique of Black bourgeois ideology," as Irene "squelch[es] the revolutionary possibilities in Clare's character."[139] It also underscores the finality of Irene's spiritual descent. Coming to terms with the fact that she had killed Clare, she "sank down" and then everything "was dark" literally and metaphorically.[140] Her downward slide represents her anxiety-induced psychological breakdown, and the darkness symbolizes the bleakness that, now magnified, has long pervaded her soul. Her efforts to play god have failed, and her empty religious rituals have not yielded the much-desired peace.

Both Irene and Helga use religion as a crutch to avoid the critical self-reflection required to develop self-knowledge and autonomy. Yet their fate cannot be dismissed as the mere effect of neuroses as structural and intersecting oppressions shape their lived experience, life chances, and access to resources. Lacking the emotional, spiritual, and economic resources to prevail or at least survive, they sink into the quagmires of the modern world—Helga awaiting the birth of her fifth child and certain death in the rural South, and Irene anticipating the unknown terrors of the modern city rapidly overflowing the borders of her neatly arranged world.

This chapter highlights the spiritual struggles of two characters in *Quicksand* and *Passing* anticipating that future developments in Larsen scholarship will extend this line of inquiry to address the broader black community in her novels. For example, as West has shown, the "multitudes [in *Quicksand*] who are unlike Helga are no better off—unable to see the hopelessness, they simply live their despair in blindness."[141] Clearly, Pleasant Green's disempowered rural flock suffers from social blindness, but I would further suggest that his followers actively cultivate hope—misguided though it may be—to cope with the vagaries of the modern world.

African Americans in Larsen's novels, poor and middle-class alike, devise mechanisms for survival. In *Quicksand*, for example, women play an active role in the black church, an institution that has historically served as a refuge from racist discourses of blackness. Within the church walls in Harlem where "frenzied women gesticulated, screamed, wept, and tottered to the praying of the preacher," Larsen depicts a scenario that "closely resembles" a specifically black fundamentalist style of worship and communion.[142] This church steeped in the African American vernacular tradition serves to shield its congregants from the impersonal world outside. In *Passing* Irene devises different but equally as significant spiritual mechanisms of self-protection. Notably, she is not alone. Whenever her black middle-class friend Felise Freeland "gets the blues," for example, "it means money out of [her husband's] pocket."[143] Assuring Irene that "an expensive new frock" would similarly alleviate her own despair, Felise reveals her commodity-based cure to spiritual unrest (referred to here as "the blues") and illuminates a broader cultural emptiness within the black middle class. This "lack," which I argue is of a spiritual nature, requires further investigation, as does Claire's intriguing quip that her aunts and their racialized religious discourse "made [her] what [she is] today," making her "determined" not to be "a daughter of the indiscreet Ham."[144] Hinting at causality, Clare reveals the centrality of racist biblical exegesis in her psyche. Compellingly, Felise and Clare, along with Helga and Irene, speak to middle-class African Americans' spiritual condition in the modern world—whether they were seeking a cure for the blues, or sheer relief from restrictive religiosity.

Expanding on Larsen's astute literary works, Danzy Senna's *Caucasia* explores black female subjectivity, entertaining key philosophical questions raised by concepts of race and gender in the late twentieth century. Namely, what does it mean to be a mixed-raced woman in a racist and sexist society? How does racism work, and how does whiteness bestow privilege upon persons labeled as "white"? Senna engages these concerns, among others, in a so-called post-race moment, ultimately affirming blackness as beautiful, complex, and multiple.

NOTES

1. W. E. B. Du Bois, "Two Novels," *Crisis*, 1928, 202.
2. W. E. B. Du Bois, Passing," *Crisis*, 1929, 234.
3. See Mary Helen Washington, "Nella Larsen: Mystery Woman of the Harlem Renaissance," *Ms. Magazine* 9 (1980): 44–50.
4. "Introduction" to *Quicksand and Passing*, ed. Deborah McDowell (New Brunswick: Rutgers University Press, 1986), ix–xxxv. Quote appears on page ix. All references to *Quicksand* and *Passing* are to the 1986 Rutgers University Press publication edited by Deborah E. McDowell; subsequent quotations from this edition are cited in the text notes with the abbreviation *QP*.
5. Nathan Huggins, *Harlem Renaissance*, foreword by Arnold Rampersad (New York: Oxford University Press, 2007), 236.
6. Hiroko Sato, "Under the Harlem Shadow: A Study of Jessie Fauset and Nella Larsen," in *The Harlem Renaissance 1920–1940*, vol. V: *Remembering the Harlem Renaissance*, ed. by Cary D. Wintz, 261–87 (New York: Garland, 1996), 285.

7. Barbara Christian, *Black Women Novelists: The Development of a Tradition* (Westport: Greenwood, 1980), 53.

8. Christian, *Black Women Novelists*, 48.

9. Born "Nellie Walker" in Chicago in 1891, Larsen "grew up poor." When her biological father died, her mother married a white Danish immigrant, and Larsen was reportedly "unwanted by the stepfather and half-sister." In subsequent years as a child, Larsen spent time in Denmark; at the age of sixteen, she spent one year at the Normal School at Fisk University, and later lived in Denmark for three years. Upon returning to the U.S., Larsen studied nursing in New York City and then worked as a nurse supervisor at Tuskegee. Afterwards, Larsen was employed as a public health nurse and as a librarian at the New York Public Library. "Through that work," writes Hutchinson, she "eventually moved into the literary field just as the Harlem Renaissance picked up steam." For full biographical information, see George Hutchinson, *In Search of Nella Larsen: A Biography of the Color Line* (Cambridge: Belknap Press, 2006), 12, 2, 3.

10. Patricia Hill Collins, *Black Feminist Thought: Knowledge, Consciousness, and the Politics of Empowerment* (New York: Routledge, 2000), 18.

11. Larsen, *QP*, 67.

12. Hazel V. Carby, *Reconstructing Womanhood: The Emergence of the Afro-American Woman Novelist* (New York: Oxford University Press, 1987), 89.

13. McDowell, "Introduction," xvii.

14. McDowell, "Introduction," xvii.

15. McDowell, "Introduction," xvii.

16. McDowell, "Introduction," xvii.

17. Cheryl A. Wall, "Passing for What? Aspects of Identity in Nella Larsen's Novels," *Black American Literature Forum* 20 (1986): 97.

18. Wall, "Passing for What? Aspects of Identity," 98.

19. Wall, "Passing for What? Aspects of Identity," 98.

20. Wall, "Passing for What? Aspects of Identity," 105.

21. Wall, "Passing for What? Aspects of Identity," 98. Psychoanalytic critics, most notably Claudia Tate and Barbara Johnson, build on psychological approaches to Helga's plight. For Tate, "materialist paradigms of race and gender that typically frame the scholarship do not entirely address [*Quicksand's*] complex textual subjectivity." She thus applies Lacanian theory to the narrative and interprets Helga's self-admitted "lack" as "an illustration of Lacanian desire" (242). See Tate, "Desire and Death in Quicksand, by Nella Larsen" *American Literary History* 7 (1995): 234–60. Quotes appear on pages 253 and 242. Similarly, Johnson explores the internal and external forces that Helga navigates in the narrative. For Johnson, *Quicksand* is a "complex analysis of the intersections of gender, sexuality, race and class." Within this framework she grapples with Helga's psyche, and concludes "Helga's apparent selfishness is based not on an excess of self but on a lack of self," See Johnson, "The Quicksands of the Self: Nella Larsen and Heinz Kohut" in *Female Subjects in Black and White: Race, Psychoanalysis, Feminism*, ed. Elizabeth Abel, Barbara Christian, and Helene Moglen (Berkeley: University of California Press, 1997), 252–65. Quotes appear on pages 254 and 257.

22. Cherene Sherrard-Johnson, *Portraits of the New Negro Woman: Visual and Literary Culture in the Harlem Renaissance* (New Brunswick: Rutgers University Press, 2007), 22.

23. Sherrard-Johnson, *Portraits of the New Negro Woman*, 22.

24. Carby, *Reconstructing Womanhood*, 170.

25. Robert Bone, *The Negro Novel in America* (New Haven: Yale University Press, 1965), 98.

26. Sterling Brown, *The Negro in American Fiction* (Port Washington: Kennikat, 1968), 143.

27. Mabel Youman, "Nella Larsen's *Passing*: A Study in Irony," *College Language Association Journal* 18 (1974): 241.

28. See Lauren Berlant, "National Brands/National Body: Imitation of Life" in *Comparative American Identities*, ed. Hortense J. Spillers (New York: Routledge, 1991),

110–40; Martha J. Cutter, "Sliding Significations: *Passing* as a Narrative and Textual Strategy in Nella Larsen's Fiction," in *Passing and the Fictions of Identity*, ed. by Elaine K. Ginsberg (Durham: Duke University Press, 1996), 75–100; Catherine Rottenberg, "*Passing*: Race, Identification, and Desire" *Criticism: A Quarterly for Literature and the Arts* 45 (2003): 435–52; and Sherrard-Johnson, *Portraits of the New Negro Woman* (2007).

29. Elizabeth J. West, *African Spirituality in Black Women's Fiction* (Lanham: Lexington Books, 2011), 149.

30. Larsen, *QP*, 23.

31. Huggins, *Harlem Renaissance*, 157.

32. Wall, "Passing for What? Aspects of Identity," 98–99.

33. Charles R. Larson, *Invisible Darkness: Jean Toomer and Nella Larsen* (Iowa City: University of Iowa Press, 1993), 69.

34. See Kimberly Monda, "Self-Delusion and Self Sacrifice in Nella Larsen's *Quicksand*," *African American Review* 31 (1997): 23–39, esp. page 23.

35. Thadious M. Davis, *Nella Larsen Novelist of the Harlem Renaissance: A Woman's Life Unveiled* (Baton Rouge: Louisiana State University Press, 1994), 275.

36. Jacquelyn Y. McLendon, *The Politics of Color in the Fiction of Jessie Fauset and Nella Larsen* (Charlottesville: University Press of Virginia, 1995), 93.

37. Martha J. Cutter, "Sliding Significations: *Passing* as a Narrative and Textual Strategy in Nella Larsen's Fiction," in *Passing and the Fictions of Identity*, ed. by Elaine K. Ginsberg (Durham: Duke University Press, 1996), 75–100. Quote appears on page 76.

38. Sherrard-Johnson, *Portraits of the New Negro Woman*, 35.

39. Sianne Ngai, *Ugly Feelings* (Cambridge: Harvard University Press, 2005), 35.

40. Larsen, *QP*, 7.

41. Wall, "Passing for What? Aspects of Identity," 104.

42. McDowell, "Introduction," xxiv, n.26.

43. Michael Lackey, *African American Atheists and Political Liberation: A Study of the Sociocultural Dynamics of Faith* (Gainesville: University Press of Florida, 2007), 87.

44. Larsen, *QP*, 113.

45. Larsen, *QP*, 118.

46. McDowell, "Introduction," xxii.

47. Larsen, *QP*, 118.

48. Larsen, *QP*, 121.

49. Larsen, *QP*, 120.

50. Larsen, *QP*, 121.

51. Larsen, *QP*, 123.

52. Larsen, *QP*, 124.

53. Larsen, *QP*, 124.

54. Larsen, *QP*, 124.

55. See McDowell; Lackey; and Whitted, *A God of Justice? The Problem of Evil in Twentieth-Century Black Literature* (Charlottesville: University of Virginia Press, 2009).

56. Larsen, *QP*, 125.

57. Larsen, *QP*, 125.

58. Larsen, *QP*, 125.

59. Carby, *Reconstructing Womanhood*, 174.

60. Larsen, *QP*, 75.

61. Larsen, *QP*, 75.

62. Larsen, *QP*, 75.

63. Silvan Tomkins, *Shame and Its Sisters: A Silvan Tomkins Reader*, ed. Eve Kosofsky Sedgwick and Adam Frank (Durham: Duke University Press, 1995), 133.

64. Larsen, *QP*, 121.

65. James Cone, *The Cross and the Lynching Tree* (Maryknoll, NY: Orbis, 2011), 125.

66. Larsen, *QP*, 126.

67. Lackey, *African American Atheists and Political Liberation*, 79.

68. Lackey, *African American Atheists and Political Liberation*, 87

69. Larsen, *QP*, 34.
70. Larsen, *QP*, 34.
71. Tomkins, *Shame and Its Sisters*, 119.
72. Tomkins, *Shame and Its Sisters*, 111.
73. Larsen, *QP*, 27.
74. Larsen, *QP*, 34.
75. Larsen, *QP*, 27.
76. Larsen, *QP*, 30.
77. Larsen, *QP*, 31–32.
78. Larsen, *QP*, 32.
79. Larsen, *QP*, 34.
80. Meredith Goldsmith, "Shopping to Pass, Passing to Shop: Bodily Self-Fashioning in the Fiction of Nella Larsen" in *Recovering the Black Female Body: Self Representations by African American Women*, ed. Michael Bennett and Vanessa D. Dickerson (New Brunswick: Rutgers University Press, 2001), 79–120. Quote appears on page 103.
81. Goldsmith, "Shopping to Pass, Passing to Shop," 102.
82. Larsen, *QP*, 29.
83. Larsen, *QP*, 34.
84. Larsen, *QP*, 87.
85. Larsen, *QP*, 34.
86. Larsen, *QP*, 87.
87. Larsen, *QP*, 28.
88. Teresa Brennan, *The Transmission of Affect* (Ithaca: Cornell University Press, 2004), 1.
89. Larsen, *QP*, 28.
90. Larsen, *QP*, 28.
91. Larsen, *QP*, 23.
92. Larsen, *QP*, 29.
93. Larsen, *QP*, 118.
94. Larsen, *QP*, 117.
95. Larsen, *QP*, 109.
96. Larsen, *QP*, 130.
97. Larsen, *QP*, 130.
98. Larsen, *QP*, 135.
99. Larsen, *QP*, 134.
100. Larsen, *QP*, 178.
101. Larsen, *QP*, 235.
102. Larsen, *QP*, 187.
103. Larsen, *QP*, 236.
104. Sara Ahmed, *The Cultural Politics of Emotion* (New York: Routledge, 2004), 65, original emphasis.
105. Larsen, *QP*, 187.
106. Larsen, *QP*, 188.
107. Basu, Biman, "Hybrid Embodiment and an Ethics of Masochism: Nella Larsen's *Passing* and Sherley Anne Williams's *Dessa Rose*," *African American Review* 36 (2002): 387, 388.
108. Larsen, *QP*, 190, emphasis mine.
109. Larsen, *QP*, 235, emphasis mine.
110. Larsen, *QP*, 232.
111. Larsen, *QP*, 235.
112. Larsen, *QP*, 188.
113. Larsen, *QP*, 235.
114. Larsen, *QP*, 214.
115. Larsen, *QP*, 214.
116. Larsen, *QP*, 235.

117. Many critics have sought to define the intriguing relationship that blooms between Irene Redfield and Clare Kendry in *Passing*. In her seminal reading of the novel, McDowell foregrounds "female sexuality," asserting that Larsen "flirt[s], if only by suggestion, with the idea of a lesbian relationship" between the characters, xxiii. Examining Irene's apparent burgeoning desire for Clare, McDowell argues that "[t]he more the feelings develop, the more she fights them, for they threaten the placid surface of her middle-class existence as a doctor's wife," xxviii. While McDowell questions the significance of race in *Passing*, Jennifer DeVere Brody argues the latter "read/uce[s] the text as a tale of latent sexual passion without discussing key issues of race and class." Illuminating the intersection of race and class, Brody writes that Irene "mimics middle-class culture which often tries to isolate itself from poverty and perversion by situating itself in a relationship above and beyond the lower-class." See Jennifer DeVere Brody, "Clare Kendry's 'True' Colors: Race and Class Conflict in Nella Larsen's *Passing*," *Callaloo* 15 (1992): 1053–65. Quotes appear on pages 1053 and 1055.

118. Larsen, *QP*, 229.
119. Larsen, *QP*, 224.
120. Larsen, *QP*, 225.
121. Larsen, *QP*, 226.
122. Larsen, *QP*, 225.
123. Larsen, *QP*, 228.
124. Larsen, *QP*, 241.
125. Larsen, *QP*, 172.
126. Larsen, *QP*, 172.
127. Brennan, *The Transmission of Affect*, 119.
128. Larsen, *QP*, 172.
129. Larsen, *QP*, 173.
130. Larsen, *QP*, 181.
131. See hooks, *All About Love* (New York: Perennial, 2000); *Salvation: Black People and Love* (New York: Perennial, 2001), and *Communion: The Female Search for Love* (New York: Perennial, 2002).
132. Kelly Oliver, *Witnessing: Beyond Recognition* (Minneapolis, University of Minnesota Press, 2001, 20.
133. Larsen, *QP*, 235.
134. Larsen, *QP*, 190.
135. Larsen, *QP*, 193.
136. Wall, "Passing for What? Aspects of Identity," 109.
137. Paula Giddings, *When and Where I Enter: The Impact of Black Women on Race and Sex in America* (New York: William Morrow and Company, Inc., 1984), 147.
138. Giddings, *When and Where I Enter*, 148.
139. Jennifer DeVere Brody, "Clare Kendry's 'True' Colors: Race and Class Conflict in Nella Larsen's *Passing*," *Callaloo* 15 (1992): 1064.
140. Larsen, *QP*, 242.
141. West, *African Spirituality in Black Women's Fiction*, 153.
142. McDowell, "Introduction," xxxiv, n.26.
143. Larsen, *QP*, 219.
144. Larsen, *QP*, 159.

FOUR
On Blackness and Longing in Danzy Senna's *Caucasia*

In *The History of White People*, historian Nell Painter argues that "biologists and geneticists (not to mention literary critics) no longer believe in the physical existences of races," but they still "recognize the continuing power of racism (the belief that races exist, and that some are better than others)."[1] Put another way, scientists and humanities scholars reject race as biology while recognizing its conceptual power and enduring uneven sociopolitical effects in the United States. Even a cursory look at documented racial inequities in housing, education, employment, and the criminal justice system in America reveals racism's presence and continuing impact on populations of color.[2] Confronting race's continuing significance and systems of privilege shaping lived experience, Danzy Senna's *Caucasia* (1998) raises ontological questions about race, while illuminating how it organizes space, constitutes identities, and impacts bodies.

This chapter spotlights Senna's novel and how its mixed-raced protagonist Birdie Lee navigates the late twentieth-century racial terrain in the United States. Like Helga Crane in *Quicksand*, Birdie is a biracial woman who self-identifies as black. But Birdie's phenotypically white body belies her cultural identification, and she accordingly longs for blackness, visibility, and love while residing in a predominantly white town. Attending to Birdie's adolescent and teenage longings, this section argues for love's centrality in the novel. In chapter 1, I quote Kelly Oliver, who writes that "Love is the ethical agency that motivates a move toward others, across differences."[3] Integrating Oliver's focus on engaging difference with hooks's description of love as "care, affection, recognition, respect, community, and trust, as well as honest and open communication,"[4] this chapter opens onto a study of love and longing in intrapersonal and familial contexts. The final section analyzes affective distress in racialized space, the emotional impact of antiblack discourse on Birdie's biracial body, and her increasing deployment of *parhesia*[5] (courageous speech) to disrupt whiteness and its psychic consequences across the color line.

Whiteness studies, critical race theory, and affect studies offer frameworks for discussing Senna's analysis of segregated space and considering how racist affect circulates, attaching itself to culturally and/or phenotypically black bodies. As George Yancy's scholarship on whiteness indicates, "the power of whiteness (white supremacy) manifests itself in many forms, but it still remains whiteness (white supremacy)."[6] While such power can appear as individual acts of racism, Yancy specifies that "whiteness remains a synergistic system of transversal relationships of privileges, norms, rights, modes of self-perception and the perception of others, unquestioned assumptions, deceptions, beliefs, 'truths,' behaviors, advantages, modes of comportment, and sites of power and hegemony that benefit whites individually and institutionally."[7] Social relations in the novel illustrate how this power strives to define, contain, and dominate blackness. Yet space for agency is presented through the power of voice. Amplifying the act of speaking out against injustice, this chapter draws inspiration from critical race theory's "counter-stories" that infuse legal scholarship with voices of color to "challenge the putative colorblindness of traditional jurisprudence."[8] On narrative's role in critical race studies, Edward Taylor says that "stories can not only challenge the status quo, but they can help build consensus and create a shared, communal understanding."[9] Moreover, he writes, storytelling "makes use of the experiences of people negatively affected by racism as a primary means to confront the beliefs held about them by whites."[10]

Tapping into storytelling's subversive potential, this section suggests that Birdie longs to tell and starts to craft her own "counter-story" to disrupt negative discourses of blackness and narratives of colorblindness. Michelle Alexander pinpoints the insidious nature of colorblindness, "created by neoconservatives and neoliberals in order to trivialize and disguise the depths of black suffering in the 1980s and '90s" and argues that it has "left America blind to the New Jim Crow."[11] Unlike proponents of colorblind theory who minimize the role of race in the U.S., Birdie poignantly illustrates its decisive impact on public and private life.

Scholarship on *Caucasia* highlights issues ranging from passing to performance, and further explores how racial identity permeates characters' thoughts, actions, and feelings. According to Sika Alaine Dagbovie, "[p]assing inhibits Birdie's self-identification," but ultimately "Birdie's reflections on her own racial passing . . . reconcile her to her biraciality."[12] Brenda Boudreau also examines passing and argues that Senna's novel "explores race (both white and black) as being, to a degree, performative, even suggesting that a racial identity is a costume" that "has very real effects on individuals within a racist society."[13] Devoid of scientific value, race nonetheless intertwines itself in every area of Birdie's life. While race emerges in the novel as a social construct, critics agree that it has divergent structural and psychological effects across racial groups.

Another group of critics considers what passing reveals about identity and power in a racist society. Michele Elam, for instance, "consider[s] the performative, iterative nature of racial identity" and contends that "[i]n Senna's novel . . . passing enables incomparable epistemic insight into class and racial inequities."[14] Also examining identities in the context of passing, Daniel Grassian reads "*Caucasia* as challenging both racial binaries and multi-cultural theory" and in so doing, "envision[ing] alternatives to racial categorization by championing post-ethnic identity divorced from race."[15] Ralina Joseph, on the other hand, argues the novel's "transformative politics involve embracing blackness, not transcending it."[16] Lori Harrison-Kahan agrees that blackness is critical to Birdie's identity and further asserts that "the novel does not end with the act of 'loving blackness' alone." Instead, it "concludes with a validation of multiplicity."[17] Offering rich insights into structures of inequality, *Caucasia* takes a hard look at practices of racialization, even presenting alternative ways of imagining the self and identity.

Expanding upon this body of scholarship and surfacing the novel's countercultural values, this chapter marks hooks's loving blackness as its point of departure and reads *Caucasia* as a rejection of white supremacist values. Examining the roots of racialized aesthetics, Charles Mills writes, "The Racial Contract makes the white body the somatic norm, so that in early racist theories one finds not only moral but aesthetic judgments, with beautiful and fair races pitted against ugly and dark races."[18] Such ideas penetrated early Western culture and persist well into the twentieth century yet *Caucasia* interrupts and invalidates traditional frames for evaluating blackness. De-linking blackness from ugliness and affirming black identity as a site of complex humanity, Birdie enacts "loving blackness" in response to white supremacist "modes of self-perception."[19]

FOR THE LOVE OF BLACKNESS

Signifying on early twentieth-century passing narratives *The Autobiography of an Ex-Colored Man* (1912) and *Passing* (1929), whose African American protagonists aspire to whiteness, *Caucasia's* phenotypically white Birdie Lee "passes" but yearns for blackness. As Elaine K. Ginsberg writes, "[t]he genealogy of the term *passing* in American history associates it with the discourse of racial difference and especially with the assumption of a fraudulent 'white' identity by an individual culturally and legally defined as 'Negro' or black by virtue of a percentage of African ancestry."[20] Born to an African American father and a white mother, Birdie possesses so-called white features, yet was raised to identify as African American, a cultural affiliation that endures long after her mother Sandy "relabel[s]" her as white to elude the FBI agents Sandy believes are "looking for a white woman on the lam with her black child."[21] During Birdie's time with her mother in "Caucasia," a predominantly white, small town in New Hampshire, Birdie assumes a "fraudulent" Jewish identity but believes that her "real self—Birdie Lee—was safely hidden beneath [her] beige flesh, and when the right moment came, [she] would reveal her, persevered, frozen solid in the moment in which [she] had left her."[22] Notions of racial authenticity—the "real" underneath versus the performative exterior—get evoked and discarded throughout the novel as Birdie reinforces and rejects racial essences, but her embrace of blackness persists and remains a central feature of her identity.

Challenging the assumption that racial identity is "visible," *Caucasia* explores a phenotypically white girl whose formative connection to blackness shapes her way of being-in-the-world. Ginsberg writes that "part of the interest of narratives of racial passing lies precisely in their ability to demonstrate the failure of race to . . . manifest itself in a reliable, permanent, and/or visible manner."[23] In a similar vein, *Caucasia* problematizes the spectral aspect of "race" and challenges visual logics locating it on the body. As the novel opens, Birdie rides in a car beside her mother and reflects on being a "nobody, just a body without a name or a history" while "moving forward on the highway, not stopping."[24] She goes on the say that "when [she] stopped being a nobody, [she] would *become* white—white as [her] skin, hair, bones allowed."[25] Following her mother's instructions, Birdie tries shedding her African American cultural identity to "become" white, and allow her body to "speak for her."[26] Although Sandy stifles Birdie's connection to blackness, her daughter retains a resistant "memory of something lost."[27] That "something" includes someone—her visibly black sister Cole, and the cultural upbringing including her parents' decision to send their daughters to Nkrumah, the Black Power school in Roxbury. While her phenotypically white body speaks "whitely," Birdie's black cultural upbringing ultimately offers a critical standpoint from which she views herself and others.[28]

It is unlikely that Birdie consciously resisted whiteness as a young girl, yet her childhood aesthetic preferences effectively counter idyllic representations of white beauty that demean African American aesthetics. She reads blackness as desirable and thus challenges racial theories that represented white bodies as the "somatic norm" signifying beauty, while depicting black bodies as "ugly."[29] Articulating her earliest visible connection to blackness, Birdie reflects in her first-person narrative: "Before I ever saw myself, I saw my sister. . . . I saw her as the reflection that proved my own existence."[30] Cole is "cinnamon-skinned and curly-haired,"[31] unlike her younger sister Birdie, who has "straight hair" and "pale skin,"[32] yet Cole is the "mirror" who confirms and reflects her identity. Birdie links herself visually to Cole subsequently at a sleepover with her friend Maria Miller, who had made her "straight hair . . . curly."[33] Gazing into the tinted mirror Birdie thinks, "I found that if I pouted my lips and squinted to blur my vision in just the right way, my face transformed into something resembling Cole's."[34] Despite her "general phenotypic resemblance to the Caucasoid race,"[35] Birdie scans her own pale reflection for evidence of much-desired blackness. Dagbovie aptly writes that in this scene, "Birdie relishes her new look, which enables her to 'pass' for black."[36] Savoring the way the mirror "darkened [her]," Birdie equates darkness with beauty and her beloved sister.[37] This fleeting glimpse of her (physical) self as black "passes" when Birdie turns from the tinted mirror, but her non-normative aesthetic preferences persist.

Birdie's relation to blackness manifests itself in pleasurable and painful forms. Specifically, both she and her sister Cole, raised by Sandy ("the daughter of a Harvard professor and a socialite wife"),[38] and Deck (a Harvard-educated anthropology professor), must perform an essentialized version of black identity to fit in at the Nkrumah Black Power school. As theologian James H. Cone explains, "Black Power means black freedom, black self-determination, wherein black people no longer view themselves as without human dignity."[39] But Nkrumah stifles black freedom by endorsing narrow notions of blackness and as such, Birdie's phenotypic whiteness becomes an added obstacle to navigate. On the first day of class, for instance, one of Biridie's classmates "threw a spitball" and "hissed, 'What you doin' in this school? You white?'" A few days later, Birdie is accosted in the bathroom by a group of African American girls, one of whom accuses her of being "stuck up" and threatens to cut her hair.[40] As Joseph notes, Birdie's "desire [to be seen as black] is essentially defensive, as she learns that she will be punished, physically by the bullying children in the school and figuratively by Black Power, if she does not appropriately articulate and perform a monolithic blackness."[41] Cole promptly puts an end to Birdie's abuse by informing the students that she is black but to gain further acceptance, Birdie "learned the art of changing at Nkrumah," altering her hair to "mask its texture,"[42] buying trendy new clothing, donning gold hoops, and adopting a new vocabulary (including the term *"nigga"*) to become less "white" and conform to acceptable forms of blackness at school.[43] At this juncture, Birdie conceives of race in binaristic terms, but she ultimately develops a more complex view of racial identity. By positing Birdie as outsider at Nkrumah, where narrowly intolerant versions of blackness determine social inclusion, *Caucasia* problematizes "authenticity" as a political concept and interrogates efforts to measure black authenticity based on one's diction, earring shapes, and hairstyles.

Caucasia problematizes the hypersexualization of black women's bodies and also resists restrictive definitions of blackness. A rich critical and historical study of this topic reveals the burdens that black women have borne given systemic sexist and racist practices. Examining nineteenth-century literary contexts, Hazel Carby writes that "[b]lack women were not represented as the same order of being as their mistresses; they lacked the physical, external evidence of the presence of a pure soul."[44] External appearances presumably "reflected inner qualities of character" and "provided an easily discernable indicator of the function of a female of the human species."[45] As such, true (white) women were expected to "'civilize' the baser instincts of man," whereas "rampant sexuality" was projected onto black female slaves, who got blamed for their masters' sexual advances.[46] Racist aesthetics reinforced inhumane practices subordinating black women based on their appearance. Teasing out nineteenth-century stereotypes that justified violations of black women's bodies, *Caucasia* critiques racialized assessments of black women's physicality.

Highlighting the insidiousness of sexist and racist discourse, *Caucasia* illustrates how their corresponding worldviews shape ordinary interactions and inform daily behavior. Nicholas Marsh, for example, the fifteen-year-old son of upper-class landlords Walter and Libby Marsh, who rent property to Sandy and Birdie in New Hampshire, reproduces racist discourse in casual conversation with Birdie. When she visits him at home, Nicholas tells her about his first sexual experience and encounter with a black prostitute in Amsterdam:

> She was this fat black chick from Africa or something. . . . I heard that black girls were supposed to be good, anyway, so we bought this one. It was all right. We all took turns with her. She just lay there, looking up at us with this blank expression. But if you closed your eyes you'd kinda forget about it, you could pretend you were somewhere else. . . . I don't remember her face much.[47]

Motivated by racist myths exoticizing black female sexuality, Nicholas has intercourse with a woman he reduces to "a black chick." Reproducing the stereotype that black women signify sexual availability (i.e., he "heard that black girls were supposed to be good"), he cannot see the prostitute as a fully human being whose "blank expression" might hide complex feelings about the nature of her work and reasons for choosing it. Indeed, his reference to having "bought" her raises the specter of enslaved African women treated as property rather than people. The woman's unspecified ethnic origins ("from Africa or something") make little difference to Nicholas, who reduces her to an object, whose face he can't recall, to gratify his sexual needs.[48] Representing unreflective racism and sexism, Nicholas casually espouses white supremacist values that blind him to black woman's humanity. His lack of self-reflexivity proves problematic as he neither recognizes his racism nor acknowledge its significance within a racist society.

In a similar vein, Senna's novel problematizes and makes strange historical associations between blackness and savagery. When visiting with Nicholas in his bedroom, Birdie picks up his racist comic book and together they laugh "over the pictures in *Tintin*," which made "the Congolese into hideous caricatures."[49] Significantly, Birdie finds humor in the "absurdity" of the denigrating stereotypes correlating blackness and savagery and therefore protests, "They've made us look like animals."[50] She telegraphs her blackness with the pronoun "us," but Nicholas, unaware of her biraciality, comments, "maybe you could be colored in the right light. Better stay out of the sun."[51] To reassert the color line over which Birdie appears to hover, he then relays an offensive joke about the size of "every black baby's lip."[52] Where Birdie has blurred the line between "us" and "them," Nicholas reinforces the boundaries of whiteness by attacking black bodies through humor. As Joe R. Feagin writes, "many white and other nonblack Americans reveal their negative views and images in the ways they mock or joke about black Americans."[53] Likewise, Nicholas affirms stereotypes as racial truths through humor but Birdie refuses to embrace his joke and the caricatures in his comic book. Racial humor thus remains a problem that produces her anxious silence, and encourages deeper reflection from the reader.

Importantly, Nicholas's individual acts of racism link up to an organized system of white racial assumptions. That is, *Caucasia* shows how seemingly personal aesthetic preferences uphold a dominant system of whiteness requiring critical engagement and critique. Nicholas's racially coded remarks, for example, prompt Birdie to see the connective tissue linking his bigotry to her grandmother's racism. Pulling back from his racial musings on her skin tone, Nicholas says, "I was just kidding about you looking colored. I mean, you don't look it at all. You're—" He paused, then turned his face away as he said, "You're pretty."[54] For Nicholas, the opposite of "colored" is "pretty." He imagines that blackness signifies absence—of beauty and humanity—but Birdie silently disagrees and suddenly recalls that her grandmother, whom this chapter analyzes below, has offered her "compliment[s]" similar to Nicholas's.[55] As Yancy puts it, whiteness is a "system" that "continues to mark the white body as preferable."[56] Invested in the same racial beliefs, Nicholas and Birdie's grandmothers reinforce white supremacist values that privilege white over black. The novel thus exposes whiteness as a system while also resisting normative definitions of what race is.

Working to de-link race from color, *Caucasia* shows how deeply they intertwine in the popular mind. In *The History of White People*, Painter writes that "[a]ccording to race thinking, race and color must agree."[57] Mired in this logic, Birdie's grandmother endeavors to bond with her fair-skinned granddaughter through a "shared" whiteness and opines that Birdie she could be Italian or French.[58] Notably, the grandmother "traced her [own] family line back to Cotton Mather,"[59] "was proud of the Mather link," and "liked to remind [Birdie] of [her] heritage every time [she] came over."[60] Given her tan skin tone, "Cole was virtually ignored," while the grandmother "would pull [Birdie] close to her and say, "You're from good stock, Birdie, it still means something."[61] Sensing something "sinister" in the admiration of her grandmother, who "would stroke [her] hair and say what a 'lovely child' [she] was,"[62] Birdie realizes as a teenager—and specifically, while processing Nicholas's racially conditioned compliment—why her grandmother's attention disturbs her. Birdie reflects, "if my grandmother couldn't see [Cole's and Dot's] beauty, she must be blind."[63] Here, Birdie adamantly—though silently—reclaims visible blackness as beautiful and names her grandmother's racial blind spots. Not only can she not "see" Birdie's invisible alignment with blackness but she also exhibits bias against her biological granddaughter who happens to look "black." *Caucasia* thus represents the grandmother as bigoted and shamefully unable to understand the complexities of race.

ON SEEING BLACKNESS

Senna's novel destabilizes simple frameworks that cannot register complex nuances of identity. According to Samira Kawash, "the passing narrative . . . is about the *failure* of blackness or whiteness to provide the grounds for a stable, coherent identity."[64] Birdie's experience encapsulates this failure as dominant binary frameworks for reading "race" make illegible her multifaceted identity. She identifies as black but, as scholars agree, her blackness is virtually "invisible" to her parents, who regularly read her as "white." In Boudreau's assessment, "Birdie finds herself disappearing to her father, sensing his discomfort with her visibly white skin, unlike Cole who is 'the proof that his blackness hadn't been completely blanched.'"[65] Dagbovie compares Birdie's invisibility to the phenomenon plaguing Ralph Ellison's *Invisible Man* and writes that "Deck seems to look through her rather than at her," once her parents separate.[66] Much like her husband, Sandy refuses to engage Birdie's identity and after fleeing Boston, she often "sp[eaks] of Cole as if she had been her only black child."[67] Understandably, Birdie experiences this "invisibility" as a personal rejection that painfully displays the limits of black/white thinking.

Disrupting simplistic racial frameworks proves critical to *Caucasia*'s cultural work. One stark consequence of racial binaries is the risk of rendering invisible the mixed-raced body, a state that Birdie experiences as unloveability. As discussed above, bell hooks describes love as a mixture of "ingredients" including recognition, respect, and communication,[68] attitudes and actions antithetical to Sandy's interactions with her daughter. A key scene illustrating Sandy's inability to recognize Birdie (whom she refers to as "Jesse" in New Hampshire) takes place while lying in bed beside her daughter, who disliked sleeping alone in the Marshes' new cottage. In a critical moment, Sandy "snubbed out her cigarette and rolled over to face [her]," and Jesse muses, "[s]omething sad had crossed her mind, and she brushed the hair out of my eyes. She was staring at me intensely, with a kind of anguished hunger. I knew it wasn't me she was seeing. I rolled over so that I had my back to her."[69] Keenly aware that her mother's heart is with Cole, her visibly black daughter who moved with Deck to Brazil, Jesse realizes her mother cannot see her as a culturally black girl who profoundly misses and loves her sister and father.

Discounting the value of honest conversation, a critical component of hooks's conception of love, Sandy prioritizes Jesse's compliance with her authority. Specifically, she insists that Jesse withhold her actual identity from her new classmates and she reacts poorly when Jesse responds:

> "Okay, Mum. I got it. I'm the daughter of a dead Jewish intellectual. My name's Jesse Goldman. I never heard of anyone called Deck or Cole Lee, and we never lived in Boston and you never—"
>
> I felt her hand slap my mouth, clamping it tight. A stinging on my lips. I wondered it there'd be a mark in the morning.[70]

Literally stifling an honest exchange and flow of feelings, Sandy fails dramatically to build with her daughter a relationship rooted in trust and understanding. Silencing Jesse's speech further distances mother from daughter and discourages the latter from stating her needs in a loving encounter. While Birdie's "hidden" blackness makes her invisible to her parents, it simultaneously gives her strategic insight into the workings of whiteness.

According to George Lipsitz, "[w]hiteness is everywhere in U.S. culture, but it is very hard to see."[71] He goes on to suggest, "[a]s the unmarked category against which difference is constructed, whiteness never has to speak its name, never has to acknowledge its role as an organizing principle in social and cultural relations."[72] Yancy further observes that "people of color are necessary to the project of critically thinking through whiteness, especially as whiteness has the potential of becoming a narcissistic project that elides its dialectical relationship with people of color."[73]

A young woman who describes herself as "black . . . a mixed girl,"[74] Jesse (as Birdie is known outside of Boston) is well positioned to critically analyze how whiteness operates in small-town New Hampshire, a racialized space in which black bodies are simultaneously rendered invisible (i.e., discounted in their complexity) and hypervisible (contradicting the norm of whiteness). According to Yancy, black bodies "have been stereotyped, criminalized, and rendered invisible by the white gaze."[75] At the same time, "[i]n the case of hypervisibility, the Black body becomes excessive."[76] Yancy's framework helps explain white students' objectification of the two African American students at Jesse's school. While Jesse looks on in silent discomfort, she listens to her new friends' discourse on blackness and witnesses the representational power of whiteness. Specifically, browned-skinned and mixed-raced Samantha is both unseen and seen through a distorted racial lens: she is invisible to white students who do not see *her*. Instead, her visual difference prompts Mona, Jesse's white friend, to view her alternately as "disgusting," "'Wilona,'" "Chunky Monkey," "Big butt," and "Samanthapantha."[77] These seemingly disconnected images draw on a long and sordid history of black stereotypes. Namely, Wilona—Florida and James Evans's sassy black neighbor on *Good Times*—evokes a constellation of negative images ascribed to black women,[78] while the monkey slur evokes racist discourse that links African Americans to apes and casts doubt on black humanity. The "big butt" reference harkens back to whites' exploitation and exoticization of Sarah Baartman, a young African woman stigmatized for her steatopygia, and inhumanely displayed in a cage in London and Paris.[79] As Jesse observes how "the girls ignored Samantha with an active distaste,"[80] she seemingly follows the advice bestowed by her father: "Study them, Birdie. And take notes. Always take notes."[81] Mentally making notes on the ways of whiteness, Jesse files away observations that ultimately shape her critical understanding of race.

Race intersects with class and gender to shape representations of whiteness in *Caucasia*. Emphasizing Mona's working-class status, Jesse gains broader insight into white racial frameworks in New Hampshire. She is careful to note, for instance, that Mona lives "in a trailer with her mother" who works in a factory,[82] and that during her exposure to "trailer life,"[83] Jesse routinely hears Mona and her family speak "those inevitable words": "nigga, spic, fuckin' darkie."[84] The inevitability of racist discourse in family conversations suggests its common usage and reveals longstanding links between identity and power—a relation that W. E. B. Du Bois describes as a "sort of public and psychological wage" of whiteness.[85] By "wage," Du Bois refers to benefits that white skin yields in public and the internal dividends for those identified as white, whether they are rich or poor. More recently in her study of whiteness, Claudia Rankine writes that "poor working class white people . . . understand our white supremacist frame is the one location where they have automatic value given their economic disenfranchisement."[86] Positioning themselves to benefit from structural privilege, Mona and her family display a failure of courage and imagination that would permit them to envision equalitarian relations rooted in common humanity. Without their whiteness, one wonders, who would they be?

Continuing her "studies" at school, Jesse witnesses Mona repeatedly dehumanize and sexualize Samantha on account of her race and gender. She further determines that Mona spreads rumors about Samantha because she "not only received the attention which Mona craved from the boys, but also she was majorette in the school band, a position Mona had wanted."[87] For revenge, Mona leverages lewd stereotypes about black women and "makes up stories about Samantha" participating in illicit sexual behavior with the "whole high-school football team."[88] Jesse watches and understands how Mona's identity as a normative working-class white girl hinges on reproducing myths about black women's aberrant sexuality. Accordingly, Mona circulates "in public" an array of offensive rumors to further marginalize Samantha's black body.[89] Jesse takes mental "notes" on whiteness but remains a silent witness to Mona's gossip mongering. She seemingly withholds her voice in opposition rather than corroborate vicious rumors about Samantha, but in merely "look[ing] away,"[90] Jesse condones her racist behavior.

According to Yancy, the "power of white scopophilia, with all its psychosexual overtones, raises significant issues regarding dehumanization, control, fear, [and] anxiety."[91] This model of deriving pleasure from looking through a racialized lens characterizes white students' response to Samantha and also Stuart, the lone African American boy at school, whom they subject to racial assumptions about the black male body. "As the racist reasoning goes," writes Yancy, "Black bodies" are assumed to have "unique physical stamina and athletic prowess."[92] Yancy further describes how "White America has bombarded [him] and other Black males with the 'reality' of [their] dual hypersexualization: '"you are a sexual trophy and a certain rapist."'"[93] Invoking similar assumptions, the white students greet Stuart, newly drafted for the football team. Jesse observes that "the other boys seemed to look up to him in a way."[94] They admire him for being a "pretty good" ball player, as blacks are expected to be good athletes, but they otherwise reduce him to a jive-talking black naturally proficient in non-Standard English, "call[ing] him 'Bro' and talk[ing] in mock slang to him."[95] Unable to see Stuart as a young man from a cultural background they can learn from, they reduce him to a repository of stereotypes. As expected, Mona also invokes racial stereotypes to make his black body intelligible and informs Jesse, "I've never known any black guys, just Samantha. Wonder if they got big dicks, like everybody says."[96] Later in the novel, Mona wonders for a second time about the size of his genitals and the subsequent fear he might inspire in unsophisticated sexual partners.[97] These racist reactions reveal a desire to define and fix rather than engage the Other. Stuart's self-perception and intentionality notwithstanding, he becomes a signifying presence of white racist fantasies.

Jesse watches silently but critically, and realizes that whiteness continually evokes blackness in the whitest of spaces. She attends a predominately white school yet her friends continually "obsess[s] about race."[98] Although her "grandmother in Boston used to say that 'the Negros should stop obsessing about race. Then maybe everybody else would,'"[99] Jesse muses, "I was finding in New Hampshire, the white folks needed no prompting. It came up all the time, like a fixation, and there was nothing I could do to avoid it."[100] Her keen assessment of pervasive racist discourse across lines of class and gender reveals its fundamental dependence upon blackness as reproduced through racial slurs, stereotypes, and jokes.

AFFECTING BODIES IN BLACK AND WHITE

Exploring how affects flow between human subjects, Teresa Brennan writes "the transmission of affect means, that we are not self-contained in terms of our energies."[101] Rather, one is continually receiving impressions from others. She goes on to claim that, "[b]y means of . . . projection, one believes oneself detached from him or her, when one is, in fact, propelling forward an affect that he will experience as rejection or hurt."[102] This circuit of affect plays a critical role in *Caucasia* as white judgment impacts non-white bodies and the black-identified Birdie. Put another way, subjects of the white gaze feel the burden of racist impressions in the atmosphere, which eight-year-old Birdie experiences firsthand with her father at the Public Gardens in Boston. While relaxing with Deck on the grass, she notices an older white couple "watched [her], frowning, as [she] went up to the hot-dog cart and made [her] purchase."[103] The older couple continued watching Birdie and Deck, finally summoning two on-duty police officers who approached Birdie and asked if "the man [had] touch[ed] her funny."[104] Judged by the white gaze as "criminal," Deck's identity as father and professor of anthropology is not only invisible; it gets erased. As Yancy observes, "whiteness comes replete with its assumptions for what to expect of a Black body . . . how dangerous and unruly it is, how unlawful, criminal, and hypersexual it is."[105] Perpetuating this racialized logic, the white policemen assume Deck is a child molester holding a white girl captive. In vain, he affirms his innocence, showing the authorities his identification card from Boston University and a photograph previously taken with Birdie and Cole. But the police disregard such documentation, much like slave catchers might have discounted a black man's certificate of freedom in the nineteenth century. The police "ey[e] [Birdie] with concern,"[106] but ultimately withdraw, unable to confirm their racist assumptions.

Birdie and her father feel terrorized at the Gardens and also bear the physical effects of their encounter with the police. In a word, Birdie feels "ashamed." She "understood what was going on, even if [she] couldn't explain it at the time, and [her] skin was tingling all over like the prickle of salt water when you stay in the ocean too long."[107] Moreover, she feels "sick and a little dizzy."[108] Observing her father during the exchange, Birdie notes that "his voice shook" when he asked the police if there was a problem, and she could "feel his fear from where [she] stood."[109] Silvan

Tomkins associates this sort of fear with "pounding of the heart" and the sensation that "some sort of information is entering our system at a rate characterized as 'too much, too fast.'"[110] Impacting both the psychology and biology, fear "is very toxic even in small doses" and "designed for emergency motivation of a life-and-death significance."[111] Reading his encounter with the police as an emergency in which his life is potentially at stake, Deck is justifiably afraid. The policemen's suspicion and bigotry, carrying the force not only of their legal authority but also the power and hatred of systemic racism, thus becomes the fear and anxiety of father and daughter. Expressing himself more freely in the car during the drive home, Deck ruminates, "And they wonder why we want to get out of this place. I mean . . . it's everywhere I go. Everywhere."[112] While Deck's failures as a parent (elsewhere in the novel) render him largely unsympathetic, his encounter with the police offers insight into how racist affect impacts the mind and body within a racist society. For Deck, as for Birdie, whiteness is "everywhere," a pervasive force stalking his steps and delimiting his freedom.[113]

While Birdie is phenotypically white, she remains "grounded in blackness,"[114] and thus responds affectively, much like her father, to anti-black racism. As Brennan argues, human subjects *feel* the affects directed toward them. Consequently, Birdie feels "sick" when the police antagonize her father; and later in New Hampshire when Nicholas expresses his disgust for blackness by warning "Jesse" to "stay out of the sun" and sharing a racist joke about black infants,[115] she "felt a constriction in [her] chest as he spoke."[116] Within moments, her "breathing was coming out funny, in irregular wheezes" and longs to 'be outside . . . where [she] could breathe."[117] While Nicholas intends to channel the negative affect of contempt toward blacks and away from his (and Jesse's) "white" bodies, she intercepts his negative judgment and registers his disdain as asthma-inducing anxiety. Reinforcing the bodily impact of racist affect, Birdie's/Jesse's encounters with the police and Nicholas capture the racial other's vulnerability to white supremacist forces.

Robin DiAngelo writes that "whiteness itself refers to the specific dimensions of racism that serve to elevate white people over people of color."[118] Inherently antithetical to egalitarian expressions of love, whiteness manifests itself as a relation of dominance that resists acceptance and recognition of the other. As illustrated above, the police officers criminalize the black male body by associating it with sexual deviance; Nicholas denigrates black women and mocks African American features; and Birdie's aristocratic grandmother tries to wish away her blackness. These white characters reproduce racial scripts rather than recognize black humanity, while love requires a willingness to engage difference. As Oliver writes, "[l]ove is an openness to others."[119] Where whiteness closes itself off, love is an open stance of humility that acknowledges common dignity, enables honest communication, and allows genuine human encounters to develop.

SPEAKING OUT AND SELF-LOVE

In a 2002 interview with Claudia M. Milian Arias, Senna states that people usually view her as white and so she has "been witness to what white people say and do when they think they're alone."[120] She goes on to make an important link between voice and empowerment:

> As a child, I heard especially blatant expressions of racism in Boston. I was struck even at a very young age by the two faces I saw white people wear: the face they wore in mixed company, and the face they wore when they thought they were alone. . . . When I remain in the position of a spy, remain silent in these circumstances, I only feel pain. . . . It is only when I cease to be a spy, and find the courage to speak out, to break the in-group comfort zone, to "out" myself, do I feel my position is a blessing . . . I've learned that invisibility only has power when you disrupt it in some way, by speaking out, airing dirty laundry, disrupting comfort zones.[121]

For Senna, "speaking out" is a form of agency that can potentially disrupt master narratives of race.[122] Silence, on the other hand, is "painful," much like "Jesse's" quiet discomfort in Nicholas's and Mona's presence. Part of Birdie's journey involves finding her voice to "speak out" against racist assumptions and resist social erasure by telling her own story.

After years of silence, Birdie's longing to reclaim her gendered and racial identity emboldens her to authorize her voice and start shaping her own narrative. Barbara Rowland-Serdar and Peregrine Schwartz-Shea argue that "reclaiming and telling one's story" are critical steps toward empowerment, "a process in which women come to believe in their ability 'to construct, and take responsibility for, [their] gendered identity, [their] politics, and [their] choices.'"[123] As the following section argues, in reassembling the scattered dimensions of her life, Birdie approaches greater insight into her identity as a mixed-race young woman, and recognizes the importance of choosing speech over silence.

Underscoring the power of voice, the novel privileges *parhesia* as a sign of maturity. As a critical step toward honoring her speech, Birdie confronts her mother in New Hampshire about why they remain in "Caucasia" where she must perform whiteness and stifle her black identity. Having left Boston five years earlier, Sandy had always assured Birdie that they would go underground temporarily until they could reunite with Cole and Deck. However, one day Birdie discovers that Sandy has hidden a postcard sent from Deck's sister, Dot, who inquires about their well-being. As her mother "hadn't mentioned it to [her], Birdie feels "cold" and "suspicious" of her mother,[124] who "had withheld vital information from [her]—information that might help [them] find Cole and [her] father,"[125] and allow her to reclaim the fullness of her identity and family.

Birdie further asserts herself following a trip to New York, where she observes a group of diverse teenagers dancing to music that "was somehow familiar, something [she] had known once long ago."[126] Realizing "how long [she had] been away," Birdie "felt like [she] had missed some great party and was now hearing about it the day after."[127] Reminded of the distant sounds and culture of her childhood, she feels "disappointment and envy" at what she had "missed."[128] Shortly thereafter, she confronts and interrogates her mother: "What the hell is going on, Mum? Why are we here?" Importantly, Birdie's "voice surprised [her]. It sounded different—angry, adult, scolding."[129] Rejecting the code of silence imposed by her mother, Birdie uses her "adult" voice that bears the mark of maturity, righteous indignation, and courage, to challenge her mother's authority. Bold and yet vulnerable, Birdie persists, speaking about Cole, "She was your favorite. Wasn't she? You loved her the best. Both you and Papa did. She was the one you both wanted to keep."[130] Truthful self-expression helps Birdie come to terms with the fact that "Cole was the one [her father and mother] had fought for, not [her]."[131] While Sandy denies the favoritism, she responds that "[h]aving a black child made me see things differently. . . . It hurts to see your baby come into a world like this, so you want to change it."[132] Suggesting that Cole is "her only black child," Sandy further denies and appears oblivious to Birdie's multilayered racial identity. After confronting her mother and then encountering at a party Samantha, who momentarily "appeared as [her] sister" and apparently informs Birdie, "I'm black. Like you,"[133] Birdie departs for Boston to reclaim the lost parts of herself.[134] Directing for the first time her own path, Birdie disentangles from the tendrils of her mother's authority and begins crafting a new story.

No longer choosing silence as a viable option, Birdie resolves to name and speak out against white supremacist forces. After leaving New Hampshire, she confronts her grandmother, who gives her money to find Cole and Deck in San Francisco, but also subjects her to the racist lament that "[i]t was doomed from the start. Tragedy in the making. Your mother should have stuck to her world."[135] So startled that she "dropped [her] teacup," Birdie vocalizes her anger:

> I snapped at my grandmother, and my words flowed with some rage I had been unaware of until now: "Oh, please. . . . You and all your ancestors are the tragedies. Not me. You walk around pretending to be so liberal and civilized in this big old house, but you're just as bad as the rest of them. The whole world—it's based on lies.[136]

Birdie's incisive words "were aimed at [her] grandmother, but also at [her] mother, Jim, Mona, and the whole state of New Hampshire."[137]

Hard-earned epistemic insights inform Birdie's reading of these whites as "tragedies" as racial assumptions and practices distort their thinking and narrow their vision. Moreover, these individuals are situated within a broader culture of white supremacy undergirding their racist ideas and behaviors. From this critical standpoint, Birdie senses her grandmother's inauthenticity: "maybe it wasn't me she loved, but rather preferred "my face, my skin, my hair, and my bones, because they resembled her own."[138] Indeed, she concludes that "[i]t wasn't a pure love, if such a thing existed."[139] The older woman worships Birdie's whiteness but remains ignorant of her identity. Unable to love what she does not know, the grandmother fixates on whiteness and cannot develop authentically loving human encounters rooted in humanitarian values. Birdie recognizes this "blind spot" and positions herself to create a new and inclusive story about race and identity. Namely, she rejects whiteness as a site of solidarity, and forges a new relationship with her sister based on dignity and love.

Oliver writes that "[o]ur lives have meaning for us—we have a sense of ourselves—through the narratives that we prepare to tell others about our experience."[140] This point is made explicit in "Caucasia," where Birdie assigns meaning to her experience and imagines sharing it with others. Desiring to tell her own narrative, Birdie positions herself in New Hampshire as a spy in a white world:

> I had even convinced myself that my passing for this white girl, this Jewish girl, Jesse Goldman, would support my father's research. I used to fantasize that once I got back to Boston, I would write it up as a report to hand in to the Nkrumah School. I even thought up a series of potential titles for my report. "What White People Say When They Think They're Alone" [and] "Honkified Meanderings: Notes from the Underground."[141]

While fantasizing about documenting her experience and sharing it helps Jesse/Birdie cope with the necessity of racial passing and suppressing her black cultural ties, her imaginary scenario also involves voicing her own story and naming whiteness as a structuring force that affects black bodies. Identifying as non-white in this scene, Birdie imagines being rewarded for her "report" on whiteness and affirmed as a loyal "spy" who "*always* reports back to headquarters."[142] While she never mounts a literal stage, Birdie develops an ability to critically engage whiteness and finds ways to affirm her lived experience as a young woman of color.

Contradicting the myth that race is irrelevant, Birdie's lived experience and resistant voice testify to its reality shaping power. After tracking down her father in the novel's final pages, she listens with skepticism as Deck downplays race and assures Birdie that it is "a complete illusion, make-believe."[143] Having lived six years in white spaces where she habitually encountered unsolicited race talk, Birdie knows otherwise and disrupts Deck's dismissive narrative: "If race is so make-believe, why did I go with Mum? You gave me to Mum 'cause I looked white. You don't think that's real? Those are the facts."[144] Insisting on the value of her story, Birdie tells him that she "passed as white,"[145] "waited and waited" for him to return, and "kept the box of crap [he] gave [her]. But [he] never came."[146] Although compressed, this "narrative" encapsulates key moments in Birdie's experience: the abandonment, the passing, the waiting, negotiating her connection to blackness, and the painful realization that her father would not return to bring her home. Her narrative testifies to experiences of racialization, rejection, and loss, and interrupts narratives that deny race's relevance. Testifying against her father's lofty denial of race's significance on scientific grounds, Birdie illuminates how race impacts bodies in the world. She, too, recognizes race as a biological fiction, but attests to its reality as a social fact profoundly impacting her life.

This chapter suggests that Birdie emphasizes the power of narrative and that her frank speech corresponds to "counter-stories" embraced by critical race theory scholars in legal scholarship. It is important to note that Birdie's personal narrative is part of a larger history of race in America. Illuminating broader issues of what it means to be a woman of color relegated to the margins in a racist society, Birdie's story offers insights into larger structures of privilege that impact and organize individual subjects. According to Sandra Hughes-Hassell and Ernie J. Cox, "Critical race theory scholars believe that by giving voice to the marginalized, counter-stories validate their life circumstances and serve as powerful ways to challenge and subvert the versions of reality held by the privileged."[147] Moreover, "Counter-storytelling is defined as 'a method of telling a story that aims to cast doubt on the validity of accepted premises or myths, especially ones held by the majority.'"[148] Such stories have been used to challenge "traditional legal discourse," writes Victor F. Caldwell, thereby "revealing the contingency of majoritarian presuppositions, received wisdoms, and cultural understandings that have driven American legal thought."[149]

I do not mean to be reductive and suggest that Birdie employs counter-storytelling precisely as a legal scholar would and for the same purpose; instead, I make the provisional claim that her story counters "received wisdom" about race and thus correlates to critical race theorists' projects "aimed at revealing how mainstream scholarship's recounting of 'the facts' fail to account for their experiences."[150] More specifically, Birdie's experience as a racialized woman in America contradicts dominant narratives upholding racial binaries on the one hand and minimizing the role of race in social life, on the other.

Part of learning to speak out requires Birdie to examine the self who speaks. Rejecting restrictive racial binaries exemplified by narrow blackness at Nkrumah and exclusionary whiteness in New Hampshire, Birdie opts for what many critics have identified as a "third" possibility. According to Joseph, "by showing the interstitial subject's inability to fit into categories 1 or 2, the third illustrates that categories themselves are flawed."[151] Importantly, "[t]he third can produce a crisis of passing or the possibility of racial, sexual, and gender fluidity (or both). Senna resolves this question of fluidity," writes Joseph, "and the concomitant crisis of passing, by having her protagonist unabashedly embrace blackness."[152] Throughout the novel, readers observe Birdie in crisis but she ultimately assembles the various dimensions of her own identity and attains a degree of peace. After reuniting with her sister in San Francisco, for instance, Birdie sees a "cinnamon-skinned girl" on a school bus in San Francisco and reflects, "She was black like me, a mixed girl."[153] Claiming blackness *and* multiplicity, Birdie arrives at a new psychological space for understanding racial identity, one that, in effect, overturns restrictive racial categories and carves an alternative site of subjectivity from which to speak.

By clarifying her identity for herself, Birdie attains greater self-acceptance and approaches the possibility of self-love. Upon seeing the brown-skinned girl on the bus, for example, Birdie "began to lift [her] hand, but *stopped*, remembering where [she] was and what [she] had already found."[154] In stopping, Birdie reflects and remembers that she has located her sister and reclaimed her suppressed identity; as such, she can cease grasping anxiously for what she has lost. Significantly, Birdie's journey and subjectivity remain in process. After all, "[i]t was still hard to imagine [herself] settling down anywhere," even with Cole, her beloved sister who invites her to move in.[155] Despite uncertainty, Birdie's inner work nudges her closer to self-acceptance. In her words, she consciously refuses to be someone "[s]he didn't like"—that is, "[s]omebody who had no voice or color or conviction."[156] Instead, Birdie chooses to express her feelings and tell her own story, which offers insights into systems of race, class, and gender. Her story speaks with "conviction" about whiteness, blackness, and a budding love of self that embraces multiplicity and increasingly speaks its voice.

Birdie's declaration, "this is what I remember," ushers readers from page 1 of her narrative into a counter-story on race and identity in America.[157] Disrupting claims of colorblindess and equality, she highlights race as a factor that organizes space, shapes identities, and delimits freedoms. This chapter examines Birdie's encounters with racialization and details her development from silent witness to vocal subject poised to critique white supremacy. Passing for white offers valuable insight into power relations, but Birdie's silence becomes a painful burden lifted only by speech that affirms black beauty, dignity, and value.

In valorizing blackness as a site of identity, Birdie's story convicts whiteness as a system that demeans, controls, and oppresses African Americans. Reaching for readers' minds and hearts, it depicts the pain of racist affect on black bodies and the physiological dimensions of existential blackness within a racist society. Moreover, doing the work of love, *Caucasia* repudiates whiteness that strives to dominate rather than "move toward others, across differences."[158] Arguing instead for a politics of love, Senna's novel calls for recognition and respect for the other, and advocates courageous ways of being-in-the-world that privilege empowering speech, honest communication, and open hearts.

As interpersonal relations are embedded in larger historical realities, Birdie's story points to broader power structures requiring readers' attention. The grandmother's elitist history; Sandy's privileged upbringing; Deck's rarity as a black student at a predominantly white university; and police officers' unquestioned power to intimidate and harass reveal structural inequalities privileging whites over blacks. In exploring philosophical questions of blackness, femaleness, and identity in the late twentieth century, Birdie's narrative also highlights the history of race and gender relations that make possible her modern-day story. Rendering visible racism and sexism, in forms old and new, *Caucasia* pays sustained attention to structural inequities and implicates readers within these broader structures of race and gender. In so doing, Senna's novel invites self-interrogation, making an urgent case for social transformation rooted in egalitarian values and love-driven politics.

NOTES

1. Nell Irvin Painter, Introduction to *The History of White People* (New York: W.W. Norton, 2010), xii.
2. See, for example, Michelle Alexander, *The New Jim Crow: Mass Incarceration in the Age of Colorblindness* (New York: The New Press, 2012).
3. Kelly Oliver, *Witnessing: Beyond Recognition* (Minneapolis: University of Minnesota Press, 2001), 218.
4. bell hooks, *All About Love* (New York: Perennial, 2000), 5.
5. Conversations with George Yancy inspire my use of this term.
6. George Yancy, Introduction to *What White Looks Like: African-American Philosophers on the Whiteness Question*, ed. George Yancy (New York: Routledge, 2004), 7.
7. Yancy, Introduction, *What White Looks Like*, 8.
8. Stephen Shie-Wei Fan, "Immigration Law and the Promise of Critical Race Theory: Opening the Academy to the Voices of Aliens and Immigrants," *Columbia Law Review* 97 (1997): 1202–40. Quote appears on page 1211.
9. Edward Taylor, "A Primer on Critical Race Theory," *The Journal of Blacks in Higher Education* 19 (1998): 122–24. Quote appears on page 122.
10. Taylor, "A Primer," 122.
11. Alexander, *The New Jim Crow*, x.
12. Sika Alaine Dagbovie, "Fading to White, Fading Away: Biracial Bodies in Michelle Cliff's *Abeng* and Danzy Senna's *Caucasia*," *African American Review* 40 (2006): 93–109. Quotes appear on pages 101 and 107.
13. Brenda Boudreau, "Letting the Body Speak: "Becoming" White in "Caucasia," *Modern Language Studies* 32 (2002): 59–70. Quote appears on page 61.
14. Michele Elam, "Passing in the Post-Race Era: Danzy Senna, Philip Roth, and Colson Whitehead," *African American Review*, 41(2007): 750.
15. Daniel Grassian, "Passing into Post-Ethnicity: A Study of Danzy Senna's *Caucasia*," *Midwest Quarterly: A Journal of Contemporary Thought*, 47 (2006): 321.

16. Ralina L. Joseph, *Transcending Blackness: From the New Millennium Mulatta to the Exceptional Multiracial* (Durham: Duke University Press, 2013), 90.

17. Lori Harrison-Kahan, "Passing for White, Passing for Jewish: Mixed Race Identity in Danzy Senna and Rebecca Walker," *MELUS: The Journal of the Society for the Study of the Multi-Ethnic Literature of the United States*, 30 (2005): 43.

18. Charles W. Mills, *The Racial Contract* (Ithaca: Cornell University Press, 1997), 6.

19. Yancy, Introduction, *What White Looks Like*, 8.

20. Elaine K. Ginsberg, "Introduction: The Politics of Passing," in *Passing and the Fictions of Identity*, ed. Elaine K. Ginsberg (Durham: Duke University Press, 1996), 2–3.

21. Danzy Senna, *Caucasia* (New York: Riverhead Books, 1998), 128. All subsequent references to *Caucasia* are to the 1998 Riverhead Books press publication.

22. Senna, *Caucasia*, 233.

23. Ginsberg, "Introduction," ix.

24. Senna, *Caucasia*, 1.

25. Senna, *Caucasia*, 1, emphasis mine.

26. Senna, *Caucasia*, 1.

27. Senna, *Caucasia*, 1.

28. See Patricia Hill Collins, *Black Feminist Thought: Knowledge, Consciousness, and the Politics of Empowerment* (New York: Routledge, 2000). Here, I draw on Collins's discussion of standpoint theory.

29. Mills, *Racial Contract*, 61.

30. Senna, *Caucasia*, 5.

31. Senna, *Caucasia*, 5.

32. Senna, *Caucasia*, 128.

33. Senna, *Caucasia*, 70.

34. Senna, *Caucasia*, 70.

35. Senna, *Caucasia*, 128.

36. Sika Alaine Dagbovie, "Fading to White, Fading Away," 105

37. Senna, *Caucasia*, 70.

38. Senna, *Caucasia*, 24.

39. James Cone, *A Black Theology of Liberation*, fortieth anniversary edition (Maryknoll: Orbis, 2010), 6.

40. Senna, *Caucasia*, 46.

41. Joseph, *Transcending Blackness*, 74.

42. Senna, *Caucasia*, 62.

43. Senna, *Caucasia*, 63.

44. Hazel V. Carby, *Reconstructing Womanhood: The Emergence of the Afro-American Woman Novelist* (New York: Oxford University Press, 1987), 26.

45. Carby, *Reconstructing Womanhood*, 25.

46. Carby, *Reconstructing Womanhood*, 27.

47. Senna, *Caucasia*, 199–200.

48. It is worth noting that Nicholas nicknames Birdie "Poca" after Pocahontas and thus reduces her to a minority stereotype.

49. Senna, *Caucasia*, 204.

50. Senna, *Caucasia*, 204.

51. Senna, *Caucasia*, 204.

52. Senna, Caucasia, 204.

53. Joe R. Feagin, *Racist America: Roots, Current Realities, and Future Reparations*, third edition (New York: Routledge, 2014), 120.

54. Senna, *Caucasia*, 205.

55. Senna, *Caucasia*, 205.

56. Yancy, Introduction to *What White Looks Like*, 8.

57. Painter, *The History of White People*, 396.

58. Senna, *Caucasia*, 107.

59. Senna, *Caucasia*, 99.

60. Senna, *Caucasia*, 100.

61. Senna, *Caucasia*, 100.
62. Senna, *Caucasia*, 205.
63. Senna, *Caucasia*, 205.
64. Samira Kawash, "The Autobiography of an Ex-Coloured Man: (Passing for) Black Passing for White," in *Passing and the Fictions of Identity*, ed. Elaine K. Ginsberg (Durham: Duke University Press, 1996), 63, original emphasis.
65. Brenda Boudreau, "Letting the Body Speak," 62.
66. Dagbovie, "Fading to White, Fading Away," 102–3.
67. Senna, *Caucasia*, 275.
68. hooks, *All About Love*, 5.
69. Senna, *Caucasia*, 153.
70. Senna, *Caucasia*, 215.
71. George Lipsitz, *The Possessive Investment in Whiteness: How White People Profit from Identity Politics* (Philadelphia: Temple University Press, 1998), 1.
72. (1998, 1).
73. Yancy, Introduction *to What White Looks Like*, 7.
74. Senna, *Caucasia*, 413.
75. George Yancy, "Introduction" to *Black Bodies, White Gazes: The Continuing Significance of Race* (Lanham: Rowman and Littlefield, 2008), xv.
76. Yancy, *Black Bodies, White Gazes*, 75.
77. Senna, *Caucasia*, 223, 252.
78. See Melissa Harris-Perry, *Sister Citizen: Shame, Stereotypes, and Black Women in America* (New Haven: Yale University Press, 2011).
79. See Deborah Willis, "Introduction: The Notion of Venus," in *Black 2010: They Called Her Venus Hottentot* (Philadelphia: Temple University Press, 2010), 3–11.
80. Senna, *Caucasia*, 252.
81. Senna, *Caucasia*, 61.
82. Senna, *Caucasia*, 226.
83. Senna, *Caucasia*, 227.
84. Senna, *Caucasia*, 233.
85. Qtd. in David Levering Lewis, *W. E. B. Du Bois, 1919–1963: The Fight for Equality and the American Century* (New York: Henry Holt and Company, 2000), 371.
86. Claudia Rankine, "In Our Way: Racism in Creative Writing," *The Writer's Chronicle*, 49 (2016): 57.
87. Senna, *Caucasia*, 252.
88. Senna, *Caucasia*, 253.
89. Senna, *Caucasia*, 253.
90. Senna, *Caucasia*, 253.
91. Yancy, Introduction, *What White Looks Like*, 16.
92. Yancy, *Black Bodies, White Gazes*, 11–12.
93. Yancy, *Black Bodies, White Gazes*, 16.
94. Senna, *Caucasia*, 252.
95. Senna, *Caucasia*, 252.
96. Senna, *Caucasia*, 248.
97. Senna, *Caucasia*, 277.
98. Senna, *Caucasia*, 248.
99. Senna, *Caucasia*, 248.
100. Senna, *Caucasia*, 248.
101. Teresa Brennan, *The Transmission of Affect* (Ithaca: Cornell, 2004), 6.
102. Brennan, *Transmission*, 119.
103. Senna, *Caucasia*, 59.
104. Senna, *Caucasia*, 60.
105. Yancy, *Black Bodies, White Gazes*, 3.
106. Senna, *Caucasia*, 60.
107. Senna, *Caucasia*, 60.
108. Senna, *Caucasia*, 61.

109. Senna, *Caucasia*, 60.

110. Donald Nathanson, Prologue to *Affect Imagery Consciousness, The Complete Edition* by Silvan Tomkins, ed. Bertram P. Karon (New York: Springer Publishing, 2008), xviii.

111. Silvan Tomkins, *Affect Imagery*, 292.

112. Senna, *Caucasia*, 61.

113. In this and on previous occasions, whiteness circumscribes Deck's movements and he likely recalls in this moment the times he would "hunch down real low in the passenger seat" beneath a blanket, while riding with Sandy and his children through "Southie, home of the Irish, or the North end, the quaint Italian neighborhood . . . or when [they] circled the streets that surrounded the white ghetto in Brookline," 249. Forced to hide from view, for his own safety, he makes *himself* disappear. At the park, however, he is hypervisible to the police who identify his black body as non-normative.

114. I borrow this phrase from Dagbovie, "Fading to White, Fading Away,"108.

115. Senna, *Caucasia*, 204.

116. Senna, *Caucasia*, 204.

117. Senna, *Caucasia*, 205.

118. Robin DiAngelo, "White Fragility," *International Journal of Critical Pedagogy* 3 (2011): 56.

119. Oliver, *Witnessing*, 220.

120. Claudia M. Milian Arias, "An Interview with Danzy Senna," *Callaloo* 25 (2002): 450.

121. Arias, "An Interview with Danzy Senna," 450.

122. Born in 1970, Senna earned a B.A. at Stanford and an M.F.A. at UC Irvine. Like her protagonist, Birdie, Senna is mixed-race and was raised in Boston. Some of her other writings include "The Color of Love," in *The Beacon Best of 2001: Great Writing by Women and Men of All Colors and Cultures* (Beacon Press, 2001), and "The Mulatto Millennium," in *Half and Half: Writers on Growing Up Biracial and Bicultural* (Pantheon, 1998).

123. Barbara Rowland-Serdar and Peregrine Schwartz-Shea, "Empowering Women: Self, Autonomy, and Responsibility," *The Western Political Quarterly*, 44 (1991): 607.

124. Senna, *Caucasia*, 232.

125. Senna, *Caucasia*, 233.

126. Senna, *Caucasia*, 261.

127. Senna, *Caucasia*, 261.

128. Senna, *Caucasia*, 261.

129. Senna, *Caucasi*a, 275.

130. Senna, Caucasia, 275.

131. Senna, *Caucasia*, 276.

132. Senna, *Caucasia*, 275.

133. Senna, *Caucasia*, 286.

134. Birdie encounters Samantha during a party in the woods behind Dennis's (Mona's brother's) house. For an instant, Samantha "appeared as [her] sister," and during a brief exchange in which she asks Samantha what color she is, Birdie believes she responds, "I'm black. Like you," 286.

135. Senna, *Caucasia*, 365.

136. Senna, *Caucasia*, 365.

137. Senna, *Caucasi*a, 365.

138. Senna, Caucasia, 365.

139. Senna, *Caucasia*, 365.

140. Oliver, *Witnessing*, 220.

141. Senna, *Caucasia*, 189.

142. Senna, *Caucasia*, 189, original emphasis.

143. Senna, *Caucasia*, 391.

144. Senna, *Caucasia*, 393.

145. Senna, *Caucasia*, 391.
146. Senna, *Caucasia*, 391. The box of "crap" is the box of "Negrobilia" prepared for Birdie by Cole and her father before they left for Brazil. The box contained a black nativity program, a fisted pick, a black Barbie doll head, a tourist pamphlet on Brazil, an Egyptian necklace, and other items supposedly representative of black culture.
147. Sandra Hughes-Hassell and Ernie J. Cox, "Inside Board Books: Representations of People of Color," *The Library Quarterly* 80 (2010): 217.
148. Qtd. in Hughes-Hassell and Cox, "Inside Board Books," 217.
149. Victor F. Caldwell, Review of *Critical Race Theory: The Key Writings That Formed the Movement* by Kimberlé Williams Crenshaw in *Columbia Law Review* 96 (1996): 1363.
150. Caldwell, Review of *Critical Race Theory*, 1370.
151. Joseph, *Transcending Blackness*, 68.
152. Joseph, *Transcending Blackness*, 68.
153. Senna, *Caucasia*, 413.
154. Senna, *Caucasia*, 413, my emphasis.
155. Senna, *Caucasia*, 411.
156. Senna, *Caucasia*, 408.
157. Senna, *Caucasia*, 1.
158. Oliver, *Witnessing*, 218.

Conclusion

In "A Narrative of the Interesting Origins and (Somewhat) Surprising Developments of African-American Print Culture," Frances Smith Foster writes that African-American print culture "became a primary tool in constructing African America, in ensuring the protection and progress of the 'race' or the 'nation' not only in defending themselves from libelous or ignorant attacks by other Americans but even more for reconstructing individual and group definitions and for advocating behaviors and philosophies that were positive and purposeful."[1] While some scholars interpret African American print culture's emergence as a largely defensive response to slavery and calumny, Foster shifts readers' attention to how black Americans employed print to record their worldviews, philosophies, histories, and experiences, as well as to document those ideas "most precious to their own psychic and spiritual (as well as physical or political) survival."[2] Attentive to psychic and spiritual concerns among others, the texts I have analyzed record aspects of African American life, while offering philosophical reflections on love's pertinence in personal, communal, and political contexts. Fleshing out these reflections, this chapter illuminates the contours of radical love in the writings of Harper, Collins, Larsen, and Senna, and spotlights affective and philosophical threads linking their texts.

In bringing together the cultural production of four writers, I do not mean to simplify the relation between texts published in different periods by authors from diverse social and regional backgrounds. Rather, I suggest that these writings intersect and enable fruitful textual convergences highlighting a broader philosophy of love that privileges compassionate and antiracist modes of being-in-the-world. Harper, for example, a free middle-class black woman whose antiracist politics align with her antebellum writings, published "The Two Offers" with an emphasis on antislavery, temperance, and women's rights. Her short story articulates a politics of love that displaces selfish individualism, imbuing the heroine with a spirit of compassion, and the desire to aid the oppressed. Promoting an interpersonal practice entailing mercy, compassion, and care for others, "The Two Offers" posits Jeanette as a model for nineteenth-century readers to emulate.

Both Harper and Collins published with the *Christian Recorder* and promote racial uplift, feminist, and temperance values. I have argued that Collins's novel draws attention to the tragic sociopolitical effects of whiteness, while emphasizing black humanity and potentiality at the end of the Civil War. Further, *The Curse* endorses mercy and care as viable responses to suffering and social ills, while privileging values of inclusivity and egalitarianism over racism and classism. The novel has its blind spots—perhaps stemming from Collins's middle-class bias as I argue in chapter 2—but ultimately champions the love ethic, and thus calls for a compassion-driven politics urgently needed within and beyond its textual borders.

By contrast, love evades the protagonists in Larsen's novels *Quicksand* and *Passing*, leaving an absence underscoring the profound need for intimate relations in a racialized, alienating world. While the thirteenth amendment abolished slavery in 1865, structural and cultural racism, compounded by sexism, prevailed and persisted in shaping daily life in the early twentieth century. Chapter 3 thus argues that Larsen, a middle-class writer, documents the ongoing social inequalities plaguing black life; further, it proposes that Larsen's novels be read with attention to the ways middle-class black women mired in oppressive systems of race and gender negotiate their own powerlessness and strive to become spiritually fulfilled agents.

Expanding upon the concerns addressed by Harper, Collins, and Larsen, Senna's late twentieth-century novel raises ontological questions about race to examine how it continues impacting bodies, identities, and space in what has been inaccurately labeled as a post-racial period. Documenting Birdie's love of blackness, the novel upends white supremacist values denigrating African Americans, theorizes the limits of whiteness, and explores existential blackness in a racist society. Further detailing Birdie's experiences as a phenotypically white but culturally black girl who observes the ways of whiteness, *Caucasia* highlights the history of race in America to show how individual racist acts merely reflect and reinforce structural oppression whose roots can be traced to the nation's founding documents. In sharing Birdie's compelling counter-story, which disrupts dominant racial narratives, the novel calls for mutuality, understanding, and love across difference.

Read together, these four texts offer key philosophical reflections on love's sociopolitical power. Put another way, racism has spawned an array of oppressive practices in America, including dispossession, subjugation, marginalization, exclusion, and extra-judicial killings. As such, Harper, Collins, Larsen, and Senna address some of the psychic and somatic consequences of anti-black racism. Mindful of the pain that discriminatory practices produce, the texts that I have analyzed attend to love's role in the politics of surviving and thriving. In the texts featured in this study, love emerges not as a sentimental notion but rather as a conscious (and conscientious) act tethered to social action. Harper thus depicts Jeanette's kindly care as not merely a personal gesture directed toward ailing relatives but also as a political act targeting the institution of slavery. Meanwhile, a number of Collins's characters cultivate a transgressive love for the outcast and thus call for compassionate social justice. Larsen's and Senna's novels reveal whiteness as antipodal to love, as white supremacy endeavors to oppress, define, and control Others. At the same time, Senna's text posits as political Birdie's countercultural love of blackness, for it counters racist values and reinforces black dignity.

Affects further unite "The Two Offers," *The Curse of Caste*, *Quicksand*, *Passing*, and *Caucasia*, as each represents black suffering and invites reader empathy in response to characters' pain. In chapter 2 I quote Wolfgang Iser, who writes that something happens to us during the reading process.[3] Specifically, the "author's aim . . . is to convey the experience and, above all, an attitude toward that experience. Consequently, 'identification' is not an end in itself, but a stratagem by means of which the author stimulates attitudes in the reader."[4] Drawing on Iser's theory, I suggest the authors that I have discussed seek to establish an affiliation between readers and texts, and also strive to shape readers' feeling toward textual content. Harper thus depicts the "trembling" fugitive slave seeking freedom as worthy of humane aid; Collins renders the psychic and physical effects of white supremacist practices to produce indignant and sympathetic readers; and Larsen calls attention to the ways racist affect impacts the black body, as does Senna, who shows how racist power and hate, directed toward blacks, become palpable black fear and anxiety. These scenes of emotional and physical distress underscore black humanity and thus position readers to respond alternately with outrage, sympathy, and empathy. In so doing, these texts promote reader resistance to oppression that may well flower into social action.

African American women activists and writers have a rich history of testifying to black humanity and documenting social and political realities shaped by race. From Sojourner Truth and Maria W. Stewart to Frances Harper and Danzy Senna, among others, black women have brought a rich intellectual and creative tradition to bear on a range of social injustices in America. In the twenty-first century, black women continue grappling with racism, sexism, and classism (as well as other -isms not addressed in this book, including heterosexism, ableism, and ageism), spotlighting the impact of racism on black lives. This book focuses on textual representations of African American pain and suffering in environments shaped by race, and explores the philosophies of love articulated by four black women writers. But black women activists and scholars have called attention to a range of oppressive practices that exceeds the scope of this book yet also require radical loving attention.

Kimberle Crenshaw's TED Talk, "The Urgency of Intersectionality" argues that we must acknowledge racism's painful consequences, including the rarely discussed topic of police violence against black women. While news stories rightly document the names of black men whose lives have been ended prematurely by agents of the state, incidents of police violence against black women have been largely ignored. Crenshaw thus asks, "Why is it that their lost lives don't generate the same amount of media attention and communal outcry as the lost lives of their fallen brothers?" [5] To raise awareness of the fallen sisters, Crenshaw has initiated a "roll call" so that audience members can speak the name of each black woman executed by the police. But she goes on to assert that

> saying her name is not enough. We have to be willing to do more. We have to be willing to bear witness, to bear witness to the often painful realities that we would just rather not confront, the everyday violence and humiliation that many black women have had to face, black women across color, age, gender expression, sexuality and ability. [6]

The bearing of witness that Crenshaw invites requires the "loving eyes" that enable authentic human encounters. We must look with openness and empathy so that we can be touched and transformed by the pain of those whose loved ones have been taken. The philosophies of love culled from the writings I have discussed invite readers to be changed by their textual encounters. Further, they help us envision a new way of reading, one built upon frameworks of social justice and love that call readers to engage and enact change in the social world.

Looking beyond the works of Harper, Collins, Larsen, and Senna to the twentieth-century writings of Lorraine Hansberry, Sherley Anne Williams, Audre Lorde, Alice Walker, and Toni Morrison, for example, one encounters narratives engaging racism, sexism and classism, as well as homophobia, colorism, and ageism. In particular, works like *Raisin in the Sun*, *Dessa Rose*, *The Color Purple*, and *Beloved* highlight the pain that racism spawns, the suffering that marginalization produces, and the profound need for love of self and others labeled by society as non-normative based on race, gender, class, sexuality, age, and/or religion. In so doing, these poignant texts confront reading audiences with difference and challenge readers to reflect on the biases they may harbor.

In "The Master's Tools Will Never Dismantle the Master's House," Lorde notes: "[r]acism and homophobia are real conditions of all our lives in this place and time. *I urge each one of us here to reach down into that deep place of knowledge inside herself and touch that terror and loathing of any difference that lives there. See whose face it wears.*"[7] Lorde spoke those words in 1980 but they resonate now as they did then, beckoning readers to look at and beyond the words on the page, and engage in self-examination. Moreover, Lorde's invitation positions us to interrogate how we perpetuate forms of oppression in our livingness, and to consider how we are located within larger systems of race, class, and gender.

The writings highlighted in this book, ranging from the nineteenth to the late twentieth century, do similar cultural work, inviting readers to consider the social world beyond the text and practice alternative ways of being-in-the-world. Critiquing racism, sexism, classism, and variously promoting multiplicity, equality, and justice, Harper, Collins, Larsen, and Senna challenge the status quo and call for a new set of values that challenge the ethos of possessive liberal individualism. Instead endorsing such qualities as compassion and mercy, together these texts emphasize a philosophy of love that honors humanity in its complex diversity. *Politics and Affect* focuses on four black women writers, but their generative texts speak to black women's longstanding and continuing commitment to social justice in the twenty-first century.

Drawing on the wisdom of black women writers and applying it to ongoing struggles prepare us to engage in the political labor that Crenshaw's TED Talk proposes. In so doing, we participate in a long tradition committed to making black women more visible, and their stories more audible.

NOTES

1. Frances Smith Foster, "A Narrative of the Interesting Origins and (Somewhat) Surprising Developments of African-American Print Culture," *American Literary History*, 17 (2005): 716.

2. Foster, "A Narrative," 723.

3. Wolfgang Iser, "The Reading Process: A Phenomenological Approach" in *Reader-Response Criticism: From Formalism to Post-Structuralism*, ed. Jane P. Tompkins (Baltimore: The Johns Hopkins University Press, 1980). 65

4. Iser, "The Reading Process," 65.

5. https://www.ted.com/talks/kimberle_crenshaw_the_urgency_of_intersectionality, accessed on January 17, 2017.

6. Ibid.

7. Audre Lorde, "The Master's Tools Will Never Dismantle the Master's House," *Sister Outsider: Essays and Speeches,* foreword by Cheryl Clarke (New York: Ten Speed Press), 113, original emphasis.

Bibliography

The African American Policy Forum. "#Say Her Name Report." Accessed June 17, 2015. http://www.aapf.org/sayhernamereport/.
Ahmed, Sara. *The Cultural Politics of Emotion*. New York: Routledge, 2004.
———. "Happy Objects." In *The Affect Theory Reader*, ed. by Melissa Gregg and Gregory J. Seigworth, 29–51. Durham: Duke University Press, 2010.
Alexander, Michelle. *The New Jim Crow: Mass Incarceration in the Age of Colorblindness*. NewYork: The New Press, 2012.
Arias, Claudia M. Milian. "An Interview with Danzy Senna." *Callaloo* 25 (2002): 447–52.
Baldwin, James. *The Fire Next Time*. New York: Vintage International, 1993.
Baltzly, Dirk and Nick Eliopoulos. "The Classical Ideals of Friendship." In *Friendship, A History*, ed. by Barbara Caine, 1–64. New York: Routledge, 2014.
Barnes, Elizabeth. "Affecting Relations: Pedagogy, Patriarchy, and the Politics of Sympathy." *American Literary History* 8 (1996): 597–614.
Basu, Biman. "Hybrid Embodiment and an Ethics of Masochism: Nella Larsen's *Passing* and Sherley Anne Williams's *Dessa Rose*." *African American Review* 36 (2002): 383–401.
Baym, Nina. "Introduction to the Second Edition." In *Woman's Fiction: A Guide to Novels by and about Women in America, 1820–1870*. Urbana: University of Illinois Press, 1993.
Berlant, Lauren. *The Female Complaint: The Unfinished Business of Sentimentality in American Culture*. Durham: Duke University Press, 2008.
——— "National Brands/National Body: Imitation of Life." In *Comparative American Identities*, ed. by Hortense J. Spillers, 110–40. New York: Routledge, 1991.
Birt, Robert E. "The Bad Faith of Whiteness." In *What White Looks Like: African-American Philosophers on the Whiteness Question*, ed. by George Yancy, 55–64. New York: Routledge, 2004.
Block, Shelley. "A Revolutionary Aim: The Rhetoric of Temperance in the *Anglo-African Magazine*." *American Periodicals: A Journal of History, Criticism and Bibliography* 12 (2002): 9–24.
Bone, Robert. *The Negro Novel in America*. Rev. ed. New Haven: Yale University Press, 1965.
Boudreau, Brenda. "Letting the Body Speak: 'Becoming' White in 'Caucasia.'" *Modern Language Studies* 32 (2002): 59–70.
Boyd, Melba Joyce. *Discarded Legacy: Politics and Poetics in the Life of Frances E.W. Harper, 1825–1911*. Detroit: Wayne State, 1994.
Brennan, Teresa. *The Transmission of Affect*. Ithaca: Cornell University Press, 2004.
Brown, Sterling. *The Negro in American Fiction*. Port Washington: Kennikat, 1968.
Brody, Jennifer DeVere. "Clare Kendry's 'True' Colors: Race and Class Conflict in Nella Larsen's *Passing*." *Callaloo* 15 (1992): 1053–65.
Caine, Barbara, ed. *Friendship, A History*. New York: Routledge, 2014.
Caldwell, Victor F. Book Note. Review of *Critical Race Theory: The Key Writings That Formed The Movement*, ed. by Kimberle Williams Crenshaw et al. *Columbia Law Review* 96 (1996): 1363–74.
Carby, Hazel V. *Reconstructing Womanhood: The Emergence of the Afro-American Woman Novelist*. New York: Oxford University Press, 1987.

Carter, Tomeiko Ashford. "The Sentiment of The Christian Serial Novel: *The Curse of Caste; or the Slave Bride* and the AME *Christian Recorder*." *African American Review* 40 (2006): 717–30.

Chakkalakal, Tess. *Novel Bondage: Slavery, Marriage, and Freedom in Nineteenth-Century America.* Urbana: University of Illinois Press, 2011.

Chandler, James. *An Archaeology of Sympathy: The Sentimental Mode in Literature and Cinema.* Chicago: The University of Chicago Press, 2013.

Christian, Barbara. *Black Women Novelists: The Development of a Tradition.* Westport: Greenwood, 1980.

Cole, Jean Lee. "Information Wanted: *The Curse of Caste, Minnie's Sacrifice*, and the *Christian Recorder*." *African American Review* 40 (2006): 731–42.

Collins, Julia. *The Curse of Caste; or The Slave Bride: A Rediscovered African American Novel*, ed. by William L. Andrews and Mitch Kachun. New York: Oxford University Press, 2006.

Collins, Patricia Hill. *Black Feminist Thought: Knowledge, Consciousness, and the Politics of Empowerment.* New York: Routledge, 2000.

Cone, James. *A Black Theology of Liberation* fortheith anniversary edition. Maryknoll: Orbis, 2010.

———. *The Cross and the Lynching Tree.* Maryknoll: Orbis, 2011.

Cope, Virginia. "'I Verily Believed Myself to Be a Free Woman': Harriet Jacobs's Journey into Capitalism." *African American Review* 38 (2004): 5–20.

Crenshaw, Kimberle. "The Urgency of Intersectionality." TED Talk. October 2016. Lecture.

Cummings, Lindsay B. "Naomi Wallace and the Dramaturgy of Rehearsal." In *The Theatre of Naomi Wallace: Embodied Dialogues*, ed. by Scott Cummings and Erica Stevens Abbitt. New York: Palgrave Macmillan, 2013.

Cutter, Martha, J. "Sliding Significations: *Passing* as a Narrative and Textual Strategy in Nella Larsen's Fiction." In *Passing and the Fictions of Identity*, ed. by Elaine K. Ginsberg, 75–100. Durham: Duke University Press, 1996.

Cvetkovich, Ann. *An Archive of Feelings: Trauma, Sexuality, and Lesbian Public Cultures.* Durham: Duke University Press, 2003.

———. "Affect." In *Keywords for American Cultural Studies*, ed. by Bruce Burgett and Glenn Hendler, 13. Second edition. New York: New York University Press, 2014.

Dagbovie, Sika Alaine. "Fading to White, Fading Away: Biracial Bodies in Michelle Cliff's *Abeng* and Danzy Senna's *Caucasia*." *African American Review* 40 (2006): 93–109.

Davis, Angela Y. *The Meaning of Freedom.* San Francisco: City Lights, 2012.

Davis, Thadious M. *Nella Larsen Novelist of the Harlem Renaissance: A Woman's Life Unveiled.* Baton Rouge: Louisiana State University Press, 1994.

DiAngelo, Robin. "White Fragility." *International Journal of Critical Pedagogy* 3 (2011): 54–70.

Dobson, Joanne. "Reclaiming Sentimental Literature." *American Literature: A Journal of Literary History, Criticism, and Bibliography* 69 (1997): 263–88.

Du Bois, W. E. B. "Two Novels." *Crisis* (June 1928): 202.

Du Bois, W. E. B. "Passing." *Crisis* (July 1929): 234.

duCille, Ann. *The Coupling Convention: Sex, Text, and Tradition in Black Women's Fiction.* New York: Oxford University Press, 1993.

Elam, Michele. "Passing in the Post-Race Era: Danzy Senna, Philip Roth, and Colson Whitehead." *African American Review* 41 (2007): 749–68

Fan, Stephen Shie-Wei. "Immigration Law and the Promise of Critical Race Theory: Opening the Academy to the Voices of Aliens and Immigrants." *Columbia Law Review* 97 (1997): 1202–40.

Feagin, Joe R. *Racist America: Roots, Current Realities, and Future Reparations.* Third edition. New York: Routledge, 2014.

Foreman, Gabrielle P. "The *Christian Recorder*, Broken Families, and Educated Nations in Julia C. Collins's Civil War Novel *The Curse of Caste*." *African American Review* 40 (2006): 705–16.

Foster, Frances Smith. *A Brighter Coming Day: A Frances Ellen Watkins Harper Reader*, ed. Frances Smith Foster. New York: The Feminist Press, 1990.

———. "A Narrative of the Interesting Origins and (Somewhat) Surprising Developments of African American Print Culture." *American Literary History* 17 (2005): 714–40.

Foster, Frances Smith, and Chanta Haywood. "Christian Recordings: Afro-Protestantism, Its Press, and the Production of African-American Literature." *Religion and Literature* 27 (1995): 15–33.

Foster, Frances Smith, and Larose Davis. "Early African American Women." In *The Cambridge Companion to African American Women's Literature*. New York: Cambridge University Press, 2009.

Foster, Frances Smith. *Love and Marriage in Early African America*. Lebanon: Northeastern University Press, 2008.

Fulton, DoVeanna S. "Sowing Seeds in an Untilled Field: Temperance and Race, Indeterminacy and Recovery in Frances E. W. Harper's *Sowing and Reaping*." *Legacy* 24 (2007): 207–24.

———. *Speaking Power: Black Feminist Orality in Women's Narratives of Slavery*. Albany: State University of New York Press, 2006.

Gaines, Kevin. *Uplifting the Race: Black Leadership, Politics, and Culture in the Twentieth Century*. Chapel Hill: University of North Carolina Press, 1996.

Gardner, Eric. *Black Print Unbound: The Christian Recorder, African American Literature, and Periodical Culture*. New York: Oxford University Press, 2015.

Gates, Henry L., and David Yacovone. "Address on Colonization to a Deputation of Negroes." In *Lincoln on Race and Slavery*, ed. by Henry Louis Gates, Jr. and Yacovone, 235–41. Princeton: Princeton University Press, 2009.

Gates, Henry L. Introduction to *12 Years a Slave*, by Solomon Northup, xviii-xix. New York: Penguin, 2013.

Giddings, Paula. *When and Where I Enter: The Impact of Black Women on Race and Sex in America*. New York: William Morrow and Company, Inc., 1984.

Ginsberg, Elaine K. Introduction to *Passing and the Fictions of Identity*, ed. by Elaine K. Ginsberg, 1–18. Durham: Duke University Press, 1996.

Glass, Kathy. *Courting Communities: Black Female Nationalism and "Syncre-Nationalism" in the Nineteenth-Century North*. New York: Routledge, 2006.

Goldsmith, Meredith. "Shopping to Pass, Passing to Shop: Bodily Self-Fashioning in the Fiction of Nella Larsen." In *Recovering the Black Female Body: Self-Representations by African American Women*, ed. by Michael Bennett and Vanessa D. Dickerson, 79–120. New Brunswick: Rutgers University Press, 2001.

Grassian, Daniel. "Passing into Post-Ethnicity: A Study of Danzy Senna's *Caucasia*." *Midwest Quarterly: A Journal of Contemporary Thought* 47 (2006): 317–55.

Greeson, Jennifer Rae. "'Ruse It Well': Reading, Power, and the Seduction Plot in *The Curse of Caste*." *African American Review* 40 (2006): 769–78.

Gregg, Melissa and Gregory J. Seigworth. Introduction to *The Affect Theory Reader*, ed. Melissa Gregg and Gregory J. Seigworth, 1–25. Durham: Duke University Press, 2010.

Guy-Sheftall, Beverly, ed., *Words of Fire: An Anthology of African-American Feminist Thought*. New York: The New York Press, 1995.

Hamilton, Thomas. *The Anglo-African Magazine: Volume I–1859*. New York: Arno Press and *The New York Times*, 1968.

Hansberry, Lorraine. *A Raisin in the Sun and The Sign in Sidney Brustein's Window*. New York: Vintage Books, 1995.

Harper, Frances. "Our Greatest Want." In *The Norton Anthology of African American Literature*, ed. by Henry Louis Gates, Jr., and Valerie A. Smith. Volume 1, third edition, 466–68. New York: W.W. Norton, 2014.

———. "The Two Offers." In *The Norton Anthology of African American Literature*, ed. by Henry Louis Gates, Jr., and Valerie A. Smith. Volume 1, third eEdition, 460–66. New York: W.W. Norton, 2014.

Harris-Perry, Melissa V. *Sister Citizen: Shame, Stereotypes, and Black Women in America*. New Haven: Yale University Press, 2001.

Harrison-Kahan, Lori. "Passing for White, Passing for Jewish: Mixed Race Identity in Danzy Senna and Rebecca Walker." *MELUS: The Journal of the Society for the Study of the Multi-Ethnic Literature of the United States* 30 (2005): 19–48.

Hartman, Saidiya. *Scenes of Subjection: Terror, Slavery, and Self-Making in Nineteenth-Century America*. New York: Oxford University Press, 1997.

Hekman, Susan. "The Embodiment of the Subject: Feminism and the Communitarian Critique of Liberalism." *The Journal of Politics* 54 (1992): 1098–119.

Hemmings, Clare. "Invoking Affect: Cultural Theory and the Ontological Turn." *Cultural Studies* 19 (2005): 548–67.

Hendler, Glenn. *Public Sentiments: Structures of Feeling in Nineteenth-Century American Literature*. Chapel Hill: The University of North Carolina Press, 2001.

Hoeller, Hildegard. "Self-Reliant Women in Frances Harper's Writings." *American Transcendental Quarterly* 19 (2005): 205–20.

Holinger, Paul C. "Silvan S. Tomkins, 1911–1991." *Dr. Paul C. Holinger's Place for Parents and Children*. n.d., accessed July 7, 2014. http://paulcholinger.com/issues-and-advice/silvan-s-tomkins-1911-1991.

hooks, bell. *All About Love*. New York: Perennial, 2000.

———. *Communion: The Female Search for Love*. New York: Perennial, 2002.

———. *Feminist Theory: From Margin to Center*. Third edition. New York: Routledge, 2015.

———. *Outlaw Culture: Resisting Representations*. New York: Routledge, 1994.

———. *Salvation: Black People and Love*. New York: Perennial, 2001.

Horton, James Oliver and Lois E. Horton. *In Hope of Liberty: Culture, Community and Protest Among Northern Free Blacks, 1700–1860*. New York: Oxford University Press, 1997.

———. *Slavery and the Making of America*. New York: Oxford University Press, 2005.

Huggins, Nathan. *Harlem Renaissance*. Rev. ed, foreword by Arnold Rampersad. New York: Oxford University Press, 2007.

Hughes-Hassell, Sandra, and Ernie J. Cox. "Inside Board Books: Representations of People of Color." *The Library Quarterly* 80 (2010): 211–30.

Hutchinson, George. *In Search of Nella Larsen: A Biography of the Color Line*. Cambridge: Belknap Press, 2006.

Iser, Wolfgang. "The Reading Process: A Phenomenological Approach." In *Reader-Response Criticism: From Formalism to Post-Structuralism*, ed. by Jane P. Tompkins, 50–69. Baltimore: The John Hopkins University Press, 1980.

Jacobs, Harriet. *Incidents in the Life of a Slave Girl*. Chapel Hill, 2003. Electronic edition. Accessed January 12, 2017. http://docsouth.unc.edu/fpn/jacobs.html.

Johnson, Barbara. "The Quicksands of the Self: Nella Larsen and Heinz Kohut." In *Female Subjects in Black and White: Race, Psychoanalysis, Feminism*, ed. by Elizabeth Abel, Barbara Christian, and Helene Moglen, 252–65. Berkeley: University of California Press, 1997.

Joseph, Ralina L. *Transcending Blackness: From the New Millennium Mulatta to the Exceptional Multiracial*. Durham: Duke University Press, 2013.

Kachun, Mitch. "Interrogating the Silences: Julia C. Collins, 19th-Century Black Readers and Writers, and the *Christian Recorder*." *African American Review* 40 (2006): 649–59.

Kasper, Walter. *Mercy: The Essence of the Gospel and the Key to Christian Life*. New York: Paulist Press, 2014.

Kawash, Samira. "The Autobiography of an Ex-Coloured Man: (Passing for) Black Passing for White." In *Passing and the Fictions of Identity*, ed. by Elaine K. Ginsberg, 59–74. Durham: Duke University Press, 1996.

Lackey, Michael. *African American Atheists and Political Liberation: A Study of the Sociocultural Dynamics of Faith*. Gainesville: University Press of Florida, 2007.

Landry, H. Jordan. "Seeing Black Women Anew through Lesbian Desire in Nella Larsen's *Passing*." *Rocky Mountain Review of Language and Literature* 60: 25–52, 2006.

Larsen, Nella. *Quicksand* and *Passing*. Introduction by Deborah McDowell. New Brunswick: Rutgers University Press, 1986.

Larson, Charles, R. *Invisible Darkness: Jean Toomer and Nella Larsen*. Iowa City: University of Iowa Press, 1993.

Lewis, David Levering. *W. E. B. Du Bois, 1919–1963: The Fight for Equality and the American Century*. New York: Henry Holt and Company, 2000.

Liljestrom Marianne and Susanna Paasonen. Introduction to *Working with Affect in Feminist Readings*. New York: Routledge, 2010.

Lipsitz, George. *The Possessive Investment in Whiteness: How White People Profit from Identity Politics*. Philadelphia: Temple University Press, 1998.

Lorde, Audre. "The Master's Tools Will Never Dismantle the Master's House." In *Sister Outsider: Essays and Speeches*, foreword by Cheryl Clarke, 110–13. New York: Ten Speed Press, 2007.

McDowell, Deborah. Introduction to Nella Larsen, *Quicksand* and *Passing*, ed. by Deborah McDowell, ix–xxxv. New Brunswick: Rutgers University Press, 1986.

McLaren, Margaret. *Feminism, Foucault, and Embodied Subjectivity*. Albany: State University of New York Press, 2002.

McLendon, Jacquelyn Y. *The Politics of Color in the Fiction of Jessie Fauset and Nella Larsen*. Charlottesville: University Press of Virginia, 1995.

Mills, Charles W. *The Racial Contract*. Ithaca: Cornell University Press, 1991.

Monda, Kimberly. "Self-Delusion and Self Sacrifice in Nella Larsen's *Quicksand*." *African American Review* 31(1997): 23–39.

Moody, Joycelyn K. "Ripping Away the Veil of Slavery: Literacy, Communal Love, and Self-Esteem in Three Slave Women's Narratives." *Black American Literature Forum* 24 (1990): 633–48.

———. *Sentimental Confessions: Spiritual Narratives of Nineteenth-Century African American Women*. Athens: The University of Georgia Press, 2003.

Nathanson, Donald L. Prologue to *Affect Imagery Consciousness, The Complete Edition*, ed. By Bertram P. Karon, xi–xxvi. New York: Springer Publishing, 2008.

Ngai, Sianne. *Ugly Feelings*. Cambridge: Harvard University Press, 2005.

Nussbaum, Martha. "Can Patriotism Be Compassionate? Moral concern begins with the local, but shouldn't stop there." *The Nation*, November 29, 2001. Accessed January 17, 2017.

———. "Compassion: The Basic Social Emotion." *Social Philosophy and Policy* 13 (1996): 27–58.

O'Brien, Colleen C. "What the Dickens? Intertextual Influence and the Inheritance of Virtue in Julia C. Collins's *The Curse of Caste; or the Slave Bride*." *African American Review* 40 (2006): 661–85.

Oliver, Kelly. *Witnessing: Beyond Recognition*. Minneapolis: University of Minnesota Press, 2001.

Painter, Nell Irvin. Introduction to *The History of White People*. New York: W.W. Norton, 2010.

Paul II, Pope John. Courtesy of Eternal Word Television Network. www.ewtn.com.

"Apostolic Letter of John Paul II: On the Christian Meaning of Human Suffering."Accessed January 17, 2017. https://www.ewtn.com/library/papaldoc/jp2sa lvi.htm.

Peterson, Carla. "*Doers of the Word*": *African-American Women Speakers and Writers in the North, 1830–1880*. New York: Oxford University Press, 1995.

Rowland-Serdar, Barbara, and Peregrine Schwartz-Shea. "Empowering Women: Self, Autonomy, and Responsibility." *The Western Political Quarterly* 44 (1991): 605–24.

Purdie-Vaughns, Valerie. "Why So Few Black Women Are Senior Managers in 2015." Fortune.com, April 22, 2015, Accessed June 17, 2015.http://fortune.com/2015/04/22/black-women-leadership-study/.

Rankine, Claudia. "In Our Way: Racism in Creative Writing." *The Writer's Chronicle* 49 (2016): 47–58.

Rose, Tricia. "Hansberry's A Raisin in the Sun and the 'Illegible' Politics of (Inter)personal Justice." *KALFOU* 1 (2014): 27–60.

Rosenthal, Debra J. "Deracialized Discourse: Temperance and Racial Ambiguity in Harper's 'The Two Offers' and *Sowing and Reaping*." In *The Serpent in the Cup: Temperance in American Literature*, ed. by Debra J. Rosenthal and David S. Reynolds, 153–64. Amherst: University of Massachusetts Press, 1997.

Rottenberg, Catherine. "*Passing*: Race, Identification, and Desire." *Criticism: A Quarterly for Literature and the Arts* 45 (2003): 435–52.

Royster, Jacqueline Jones. *Traces of a Stream: Literacy and Social Change Among African American Women*. Pittsburgh: University of Pittsburgh Press, 2000.

Sato, Hiroko. "Under the Harlem Shadow: A Study of Jessie Fauset and Nella Larsen." In *The Harlem Renaissance 1920–1940*, vol. V: *Remembering the Harlem Renaissance*, ed. by Cary D. Wintz, 261–87. New York: Garland, 1996.

Scheick, William. "Strategic Ellipsis in Harper's 'The Two Offers.'" *Southern Literary Journal* 23 (1991): 14–18.

Sedgwick, Eve K. *Touching Feeling: Affect, Pedagogy, Performativity*. Durham: Duke University Press, 2003.

Senna, Danzy. *Caucasia*. New York: Riverhead Books, 1998.

———. "The Color of Love." In *The Beacon Best of 2001: Great Writing by Women and Men of All Colors and Cultures*. Boston: Beacon Press, 2001.

———. "The Mulatto Millennium." In *Half and Half: Writers on Growing Up Biracial and Bicultural*. New York: Pantheon Books, 1998.

Sherrard-Johnson, Cherene. *Portraits of the New Negro Woman: Visual and Literary Culture in the Harlem Renaissance*. New Brunswick: Rutgers University Press, 2007.

Sorisio, Carolyn. *Fleshing Out America: Race, Gender, and the Politics of the Body in American Literature, 1833–1879*. Athens, University of Georgia Press, 2002.

Tate, Claudia. *Domestic Allegories of Political Desire: The Black Heroine's Text at the Turn of the Century*. New York: Oxford University Press, 1992.

———. "Nella Larsen's *Passing*: A Problem of Interpretation." *Black American Literature Forum* 14 (1980): 142–46.

———. "Desire and Death in *Quicksand*, by Nella Larsen." *American Literary History* 7 (1995): 234–60.

Taylor, Edward. "A Primer on Critical Race Theory." *The Journal of Blacks in Higher Education* (1998): 122–24.

Thrailkill, Jane. *Affecting Fictions: Mind, Body, and Emotion in American Literary Realism*. Cambridge: Harvard University Press, 2007.

Tomkins, Silvan. *Shame and Its Sisters: A Silvan Tomkins Reader*, ed. Eve Kosofsky Sedgwick and Adam Frank. Durham: Duke University Press, 1995.

Tompkins, Jane. *Sensational Designs: The Cultural Work of American Fiction, 1790–1860*. New York: Oxford University Press, 1985.

Tucker, Veta. "A Tale of Disunion: The Racial Politics of Unclaimed Kindred in Julia C. Collins's *The Curse of Caste; or the Slave Bride*." *African American Review* 40 (2006): 743–54.

Wall, Cheryl A. "Passing for What? Aspects of Identity in Nella Larsen's Novels." *Black American Literature Forum* 20 (1986): 97–111.

Wanzo, Rebecca. *The Suffering Will Not Be Televised: African American Women and Sentimental Political Storytelling*. New York: SUNY, 2009.

Washington, Mary Helen. "Nella Larsen: Mystery Woman of the Harlem Renaissance." *Ms. Magazine* 9 (1980): 44–50.

Weedon, Chris. *Feminist Practice and Poststructuralist Theory*. Second edition. Malden: Blackwell, 1997.

Welter, Barbara. "The Cult of True Womanhood: 1820–1860." *American Quarterly* 18 (1966): 151–74.
Wesley, Charles H. "Lincoln's Plan for Colonizing the Emancipated Negroes." *Journal of Negro History* 4 (1919): 7–21.
West, Cornel with David Ritz. *Brother West: Living and Loving Out Loud, A Memoir*. Carlsbad: Smiley Books, 2009.
West, Cornel. *The Cornel West Reader*. New York: Basic Civitas, 1999.
———. *Race Matters*. Boston: Beacon Press, 2001.
West, Elizabeth J. *African Spirituality in Black Women's Fiction*. Lanham: Lexington Books.
Wexler, Laura. "Tender Violence: Literary Eavesdropping, Domestic Fiction, and Educational Reform." In *The Culture of Sentiment: Race, Gender, and Sentimentality in Nineteenth Century America*, ed. by Shirley Samuels, 9–38. New York: Oxford University Press, 1992.
White, Deborah Gray. *Ar'n't I a Woman?: Female Slaves in the Plantation Sout*h. New York: W.W. Norton, 1999.
Whitted, Qiana J. 2009. *A God of Justice? The Problem of Evil in Twentieth-Century Black Literature*. Charlottesville: University of Virginia Press, 2011.
Williams, Andrea N. "African American Literary Realism, 1865–1914." In *A Companion to African American Literature*, ed. by Gene Andrew Jarrett. Malden: Wiley-Blackwell, 2010.
Williams, Heather. *Help Me to Find My People: The African American Search for Family Lost in Slavery*. Chapel Hill: The University of North Carolina Press, 2012.
Willis, Deborah. Introduction to *Black 2010: They Called Her Venus Hottentot*, ed. by Deborah Willis, 3–11. Philadelphia: Temple University Press, 2010.
Wyatt-Brown, Bertram. *The Shaping of Southern Culture: Honor, Grace, and War, 1760s–1880s*. Chapel Hill: The University of North Carolina Press, 2001.
———. *Southern Honor: Ethics and Behavior in the Old South*. New York: Oxford University Press, 1982.
Yancy, George. *Black Bodies, White Gazes: The Continuing Significance of Race*. Lanham: Rowman and Littlefield, 2008.
———. *Look, A White!: Philosophical Essays on Whiteness*. Philadelphia: Temple University Press, 2012.
———. Introduction to *What White Looks Like*: *African-American Philosophers on the Whiteness Question*, ed. by George Yancy. New York: Routledge, 2004.
Youman, Mary Mabel. "Nella Larsen's *Passing*: A Study in Irony." *College Language Association Journal* 18 (1974): 235–41.

Index

abolition, 13, 21, 24, 25
activism, 1, 18; African-American women and, 107; as anti-slavery, 7, 24–25, 68; racial uplift as, 23–24
affect, 1; body and, 92–93; definition of, 4; of distress, 17–19, 43–55; emotion and, 4–5; model of, 6; reader-response theory and, 2, 23
affect studies, 2, 65
affect theory, 4; language of, 18; proponents of, 3; suffering and, 12
African Americans, 50; church and, 76; documentation and, 14, 105, 106, 107–108; humanity and, 6, 25, 38, 90, 93; oppression and, 68; print culture of, 6, 105; survival mechanisms for, 75–76
African-American women, 65; activism and, 107; autonomy for, 16, 26, 74; bonds between, 47; literary traditions of, 3, 8, 36, 107, 109; police violence against, 108; as single, 25–26; social practices of, 46; stereotypes and, 26, 86, 91; subjectivity of, 27, 55, 76
African Methodist Episcopal Church, 36
The Afro-American newspaper, 26
agency, 4, 70, 71; love and, 12, 81; spirituality and, 7–8, 50, 71–72; voice and, 82, 94
Ahmed, Sara, 3, 4, 49; on fear, 72
alienation, 71
anger. *See* rage
Anglo African Magazine, 11, 14
antislavery movement, 16; activism and, 7, 24–25, 68; lectures and, 13
anxiety, 63, 75, 91, 93, 107
An Archive of Feelings (Cvetkovich), 2
Arias, Claudia M. Milian, 94

authenticity, 84, 85
autonomy, 16, 26, 74

Barnes, Elizabeth, 44, 58n100
Basu, Biman, 72
benevolence, 46
binaries, 88, 97–98
Birt, Robert, 38
Black, Miss Margaret, 26–27
black feminism, 61, 64; scholarship on, 7
blackness: longing and, 81–99; love of, 83–88; relation to, 85; savagery and, 87; visibility of, 88–92, 109
Black Power, 85
blind spots, 13, 53, 74, 96
the body: affect on, 92–93; racism and, 6, 74, 89
Boyd, Melba Joyce, 14
Brennan, Teresa, 4, 71; on transmission of affect, 92
Brown, William H., 44

Carby, Hazel, 62–63, 67
Carter, Tomeiko Ashford, 50
Caucasia (Senna), 8, 76; blackness and longing in, 81–99
Chakkalakal, Tess, 20
Christianity, 64; Sentimentalism and, 52; service and, 13
Christian Recorder, 34; ads in, 48; distribution of, 36; essays in, 42; goal of, 49
church, 29n63, 64, 66, 69; African Americans and, 76
citizenship, 1, 26, 33, 53, 54
Civil Rights Act (1875), 55
the Civil War, 13, 26, 34, 50; poverty after, 68

classism, 20; privilege and, 54; racism and, 13, 41, 106, 108
Cole, Jean Lee, 48
Collins, Julia, 6; deracialization in works by, 33–55
colonization, 33
colorblindness, 82
community, 53; black community as, 11, 36, 75; in fiction, 52; love and, 23–27
compassion, 13, 19; distress and, 19; as intra-racial, 47–48; mercy and, 46; Nussbaum on, 44–45, 51–52
Cone, James H., 68, 85
connection, 97; divinity and, 64–76
consumption, 70
cowardice, 40
Crenshaw, Kimberle, 107–108
critical race studies, 82, 97
cult of true womanhood, 17
The Cultural Politics of Emotion (Ahmed), 3, 72
culture, 17, 95, 103n146; as bourgeoisie, 21; materialism and, 70; print and, 6, 105; as Western, 83
Cummings, Lindsay B., 45
The Curse of Caste; or The Slave Bride (Collins), 6, 7; Golden Rule deracialization in, 33–55
Cvetkovich, Anne, 2, 5

Dagbovie, Sika Alaine, 82, 85
Davis, Thadious, 65
death, 18, 73; of Collins, 34; healing process and, 22
DiAngelo, Robin, 93
discrimination, 16, 26, 72, 75
divinity, 64–76
Dobson, Joanne, 47
documentation, 1, 92; African Americans and, 14, 105, 106, 107–108; of experience, 96–97; pain and, 2, 6
dualisms, 3
Du Bois, W. E. B., 35, 90

economics, 55, 90; depressions and, 18; privilege and, 24, 74–75

education, 26; inequality and, 81; racial uplift and, 34, 36
emotion: affect and, 4–5; texts and, 3. *See also specific emotions*
empathy, 2, 108; definitions of, 44–45
experience, 4, 63, 107; documentation of, 96–97; empathy and, 45; as lived, 3, 7, 12, 20, 26, 68, 72

families, 47–48
favoritism, 95
Feagin, Joe R., 87
fear, 72; Tomkins on, 93
fluidity, 98
Foster, Francis Smith, 105
Frank, Adam, 5
Fulton, DoVeanna, 15–16

Gaines, Kevin, 53
Gardner, Eric, 50
Giddings, Paula, 75
Ginsberg, Elaine K., 83, 84
the Golden Rule, 33–55
Goldsmith, Meredith, 70

Hamilton, Thomas, 14
Harlem Renaissance, 61, 77n9
Harper, Fenton, 13
Harper, Frances, 7, 11–27
Hendler, Glenn, 16; on sympathy, 19
hierarchy, 37–38
history, 12, 34; historians and, 34; sentimentalism and, 44; of stereotypes, 90
The History of White People (Painter), 81
Holinger, Paul C., 6
hooks, bell, 12, 36; love conception of, 12, 42, 59n156, 88–89
Horton, James, 24
Horton, Lois, 24
humanity, 13, 40; African Americans and, 6, 25, 38, 90, 93; values and, 96
humor, 87
hypersexualization, 85–86, 91

ideology: racism and, 7, 24, 35, 50–51; sexism as, 24; true womanhood as, 17; whiteness as, 41

Incidents in the Life of a Slave Girl (Jacobs), 41
inequality, 20, 54, 81, 99
intersectionality, 90, 107–108; oppression and, 75
interviews, 94
intimacy, 46
Iola Leroy, or Shadows Uplifted (Frances Harper), 14
Iser, Wolfgang, 4, 39, 107

Jacobs, Harriet, 41
John Paul II, Pope, 51

Kawash, Samira, 88

Lackey, Michael, 69
language, 73; of affect theory, 18; power of, 21; of sympathy, 44
Larsen, Nella, 7–8, 55, 77n9; spirituality and, 61–76
Lincoln, Abraham, 33
Lipsitz, George, 89
literature, 4; devices in, 62–63; mammy figure in, 49
Lorde, Audre, 108
love, 61; agency and, 12, 81; as antiracism, 36; of blackness, 83–88; community and, 23–27; elusiveness of, 7; hooks conception of, 12, 42, 59n156, 88–89; love-driven politics and, 11–27, 27n7, 43, 54; philosophy of, 2, 7, 105, 108, 109; in public, 19–21; redemption as, 43–55; representation of, 35; self-love as, 94–99; social movements and, 12; sociopolitics and, 1; suffering and, 39, 107; as transgressive, 107; wealth as, 21
lynching, 6, 68

marriage, 66–67
materialism: culture and, 70; values and, 21–22
McDowell, Deborah, 61, 63
McLendon, Jacquelyn Y., 65
memory, 46, 95
"Memory and Imagination" (Collins), 42, 46

Mills, Charles, 34–35, 38, 83
mixed-race and mulatta identity, 8, 81; ambiguity of, 15; binaries and, 88, 97–98; tragedy trope of, 61–62, 63, 64, 65, 95
models, 27, 43–44; of healthy partnerships, 47; paternalism as, 39–40
Moody, Joycelyn, 52
Morrison, Toni, 1

nationalism, 14
Native Americans, 45
Ngai, Sianne, 5, 65
Nussbaum, Martha C., 44–45, 51–52

OED. *See Oxford English Dictionary*
Oliver, Kelly, 12–13, 96
oppression, 14, 17, 53, 106; African Americans and, 68; intersectionality and, 75; resistance to, 6
othering, 74, 91
Our Greatest Want (Frances Harper), 11, 27
Oxford English Dictionary (OED), 44

Painter, Nell, 81
parhesia, 82, 94
paternalism, 39–40
patriarchy, 54; marriage and, 66–67
phenotype, 74, 84–85, 93
poetry, 13, 14, 25
poststructuralist theory, 64
poverty, 40, 43, 67; in post-Civil War South, 68
power, 40, 72; identity and, 83; of language, 21; of narrative, 97; spirituality and, 73; systems and, 40, 93
The Power of Sympathy (Brown), 44
prayer, 73
privilege, 20; classism and, 54; economics and, 24, 74–75; materialism and, 21
Puritan work ethic, 53

Quicksand and Passing (Larsen), 7–8; scholarship on, 62–64, 75

Race Matters (West), 25
Racial Contract, 34–35, 38, 83
racial identity, 25, 65; as black, 48–49; clarification of, 98; coherence of, 88; fraudulence and, 84; power and, 83; whiteness and, 37, 38
racial passing, 63–64, 82–83, 96
racial uplift, 14, 34; as activism, 23–24
racism, 70–71, 93; acts of, 87; black body and, 6, 74, 89; classism and, 13, 41, 106, 108; homophobia and, 108; ideology and, 7, 24, 35, 50–51; sexism and, 63, 69, 86; in United States, 67–68, 81
rage, 73–74, 95
reader-response theory, 43; affect and, 2, 23
reconstruction, 45, 55
religion, 52, 66, 75
representation, 54, 67, 84; of love, 35; of slavery, 53; texts and, 4; of whiteness, 90
responsibility, 21
Rowland-Serdar, Barbara, 94
Royster, Jacqueline Jones, 26

Salvation: Black People and Love (hooks), 12
scholarship: on Black Feminism, 7; on *Caucasia*, 82–83; *on Quicksand and Passing* (Larsen), 62–64, 75; on *The Two Offers* (Frances Harper), 15–16, 16–17; on whiteness, 82
Schwartz-Shea, Peregrine, 94
scopophilia, 91
Sedgwick, Eve Kosofsky, 2; affect studies and, 5
self-love, 94–99
Senna, Danzy, 8, 76, 81–99, 102n122
Sensational Designs (Tompkins), 44
Sentimental Designs (Tompkins), 16
sentimentalism, 16, 44; Christianity and, 52; history of, 44; reader and, 22–23; relations and, 47; violence of, 45
service: Christianity and, 13; spirituality and, 23; suffering and, 17, 18; sympathy and, 22
sexism, 24; racism and, 63, 69, 86

sexuality, 63, 80n117
Sherrard-Johnson, Cherene, 65
silence, 94–95
slavery, 20; families and, 47–48; representation of, 53; victims of, 62
social movements, 1, 12
Sorisio, Carolyn, 15
Southern manhood and honor, 37, 40
speaking out, 94–99
spirituality: agency and, 7–8, 50, 71–72; Larsen and, 61–76; power and, 73; service and, 23
steatopygia, 90
stereotypes, 53; African American women and, 26, 86, 91; history of, 90; humor and, 87
storytelling, 82, 98
subjectivity, 25–26; African-American women and, 27, 55, 76
suffering, 22, 39, 42, 50; affect theory and, 12; faith and, 69; John Paul II on, 51, 59n166; love as response to, 39, 107; service and, 17, 18
sympathy, 18, 38, 49; definitions of, 44; Hendler on, 19; language of, 44; service and, 22

Taylor, Edward, 82
temperance, 15
texts: community and, 52; emotion and, 3; record as, 105; representations in, 4
Tomkins, Silvan S., 5–6, 17–18; on distress, 43; on fear, 93
Tompkins, Jane, 16, 44
Touching Feeling (Sedgwick), 2
The Transmission of Affect (Brennan), 4, 71
trust, 89
Tucker, Veta, 43
The Two Offers (Frances Harper), 7; love-driven politics and, 11–27

Ugly Feelings (Ngai), 5
United States: racism in, 67–68, 81; whiteness in, 89
unity, 44, 50

values, 15, 109; humanity and, 96; materialism and, 21–22
violence, 108; of sentimentalism, 45; whiteness and, 37–41

Wall, Cheryl A., 63
Welter, Barbara, 17
West, Cornel, 25
Wexler, Laura, 45
White, Deborah Gray, 24
whiteness, 102n113; black body and, 92–93; corruption and, 70; as cultural formation, 50–51; identity and, 37, 38; ideology of, 41; phenotype and, 74, 84–85, 93; remorse and, 41–42; representation of, 90; scholarship on, 82; system of, 87, 98; in United States, 89; violence and, 37–41
wishes, 73
Women's Christian Temperance Union, 14
women's sphere, 7, 16–17, 18, 26, 72
Wyatt-Brown, Bertram, 37

Yancy, George, 89, 92
Youman, Mary Mabel, 64

About the Author

Kathy Glass is associate professor of English at Duquesne University. She is the author of *Courting Communities: Black Female Nationalism and Syncre-nationalism in the Nineteenth-Century North* (Routledge 2006), and articles on race, gender, and pedagogy. Her recent publications include essays in the *Companion to the Harlem Renaissance* (Blackwell 2015) and the collection *Exploring Race in Predominantly White Classrooms: Scholars of Color Reflect* (Routledge 2014).